There is a current that flows through the lives of all people. It precedes the first conversation ever spoken, and it is desired by all that breathe. It is the universal rhythm that flows in and out of every human being. It is the rhythm of LOVE... The intent of it, healing some and the misuse of it, destroying others. Love is more valuable than all it encounters. May True Unhindered Love find and keep you.

OTHER BOOKS BY
Dr. Dawn M. Harvey

THE PRESENCE OF POWER
THE COURAGE TO BOUNCE BACK
EMBRACE YOUR GREATNESS
EYG WORKBOOK AND CD CURRICULUM

Get your copies today!

Order Online at WWW.DAWNMHARVEY.COM

Marriage Unbreakable

THE WAR AGAINST DIVORCE

THE
GUIDE TO
GETTING
AND
STAYING
MARRIED

Marriage Unbreakable

THE WAR AGAINST DIVORCE

THE
GUIDE TO
GETTING
AND
STAYING
MARRIED

DR. DAWN M. HARVEY

Unlock Publishing House
6715 Suitland Road Suite A
Morningside MD 20746
www.unlockpublishinghouse.com
1 (701) 484-3303

ISBN: 978-0-9967941-3-8 Paperback
ISBN: 978-0-9967941-4-5 Hardcover
Library of Congress Publication Data
LCCN: 2016951584

1. Self Help Techniques
2. FAMILY & RELATIONSHIPS / Marriage & Long Term Relationships
3. Religion : Christian Life - Love & Marriage
4. FAMILY & RELATIONSHIPS / Dating

Marriage Unbreakable, The War Against Divorce was written to be a tool that you can use in your marriage. In this book, you will find my heart for married couples and those who desire to be married. You will hear the analogy of marriage being described as an airplane and discover the role of the Pilot and the Co-pilot. You will read about the pitfalls of divorce and the importance of communication, intimacy and revealing your sexual appetite. You will find a way to develop the most intimate relationship possible and design a Love System that will explore and enhance every facet of marriage.

This is so very important to me because I found myself maneuvering through life after experiencing a divorce. It all happened so quickly. There I was divorced with two children and attempting to rebuild my life. Looking back on it now and how miraculous my life and the lives of my children are, I know that God had to have stepped in and taken over our lives.

With my corporate training experience, I launched out into the world of entrepreneurship in the fields of business development, training, coaching and personal development. Now after 25 years of simply assisting companies and individuals as they maximize their potential, I find myself sharing with you one of my most exciting projects.

I am Waging a War Against Divorce and fighting for your marriage with you. It is so important to me that you do not end up where I was. Did I make it? Yes. Have I been able to rebuild my life and sustain a successful career? Yes. People do it every day. But why build something new when you can just enhance and preserve something that is already built? I want you and your spouse to win, and if you are not married yet, I want your marriage to have a chance to last when love does find its way to you. I want you to have one of the Strongest Marriages in America. And I believe that you can.

In the battle with you,

Dr. Dawn

Table of Contents

Reviews

Dr. Dawn M. Harvey is what I call a relationship guru. Her heart for people is second to none. She has a unique approach as it pertains to love and marriage. But what really matters is that her systems work. My wife and I value her guidance and glean from her expertise in many areas.

Author and Christian Leader, Ricardo Dorcean of Kingsport, TN

Dr. Dawn saved my marriage. When I met Dr. Dawn I was not sure how my marriage was going to turn out. There were also a lot of other areas in my life that I wanted to improve. After working with her, I was able to resolve some of the issues in my life but most importantly, my marriage was restored. This book is a must read. As I flipped the pages, I wished that my husband and I had read this book before we married each other. I will also say that there is nothing compared to actually working with her. I would absolutely suggest that as well.

Happy Wife and Mother, M. Carter of Clinton, MD

INTRODUCTION

Marriage Unbreakable, The War Against Divorce is designed to be a quick, easy but thought provoking read. There are already so many books sitting on bookshelves in bookstores about marriage, relationships, and divorce. So I was not interested in writing one of those. I wanted to write about what I could not find in a book and on what I have been able to use successfully in counseling to help couples win the battle as it pertains to facing divorce and preparing individuals for marriage.

You may hear things repeated more than once to reiterate its importance, just take note of those mentions. Use the Tool Pages at the end of each chapter to aid in your communication and understanding of what both of you interpret from the content. Remember, you may not always agree, but understanding is the key. It's time to dig in....

This book is for the lovers, the fighters and the afraid. The lovers are couples who have had the courage to commit to another human being in an effort to build something that will last. The fighters are those who are searching for the strength to stop fighting with themselves and those that they love because of what they have experienced or been through. The afraid are those who do not know what to do. They have tried love before to no avail, and they have been disappointed so many times that they do not have the energy left to do anything. I have great news for all of us. There is hope for the lovers, the fighters and the afraid. There is a chance that you will meet the right person or save your marriage, and I do not want you to blow it because of the relationships that did not work in the past. Sometimes our past can lie to us about our future. So I am here to tell you that it is possible for you to finally not only get married but stay married.

I was exposed to countless situations while coaching and training individuals, companies and organizations over the last 25 years. I have done everything from leadership, customer service and inspirational training in front of thousands of people to small groups. All of these settings presented various opportunities for people to come to me and discuss their relationship issues along with many other topics. I have always been pretty good at devising a master plan and establishing direction. But I found myself being drawn to this particular topic and as a result, I landed here, "Waging a War Against Divorce" and helping couples rekindle the fire in their marriage.

Initially, I started out talking to women about their marriage in an effort to stop them from ending up in my situation. You see, some years back I found myself divorced and raising two children alone. A lot of people like to place blame on the other party. But the truth is that no one is perfect, and no one is totally innocent when it comes to divorce. Even if we are not the one largely responsible for the trauma that caused the divorce, most of us would be hard pressed to say that each of us couldn't have done something or said something better. It takes two people to be married, and potentially it takes two people to get a divorce unless there is an extreme issue like addiction, infidelity or abuse involved.

What I found as I talked to the women, was that we were emotionally driven in situations that needed rational thought. And the state of being emotional and the state of being rational are in intense competition with each other. Our conversation, our actions, and our mannerisms determined the outcome in a lot of our situations because we were not thinking; we were just speaking based on how the person or situation made us feel. As we came up with solutions for each couple, we found that the outcome was amazing and produced great results. The couples were getting stronger, and things began to take a turn for the better. Over time, I found that the husbands were very receptive to the changes that were taking place in their wives and I ended up counseling more couples than I did individuals.

Now, I find myself in a very wonderful but peculiar place. I do more couples training than I do individual women, as it pertains to marriage. The success they have experienced in rekindling or recommitting to their marriages was a clear indicator that I was on to something special. And that is why we are here together sharing the idea of love and happiness to the masses.

Love is a truth; it is a reality. Love never fails, so it is important to get you to that stage with each other first. Are you sure that it is love? It feels like love long before it becomes love. And that's why this is so important. I have set out on a mission to wage a war against divorce, miscommunication, and discord when it comes to dealing with someone that you love.

This book is the culmination of successes and failures designed to give every couple an opportunity to engage, and encounter a new relationship with some longevity and success. It is to resolve and rectify the issues in an existing marriage or relationship and give a couple that is frustrated the opportunity to stay together and grow together.

It is my heart's desire that everyone would find true love. And that in doing so, they would possess the skills and tools that they need to deal with their past, their pain, their problems, their personality and their family in an effort to align themselves with another human being and build a life by design; a life that they both would enjoy and love.

So my mission is to prevent someone's life from experiencing what I have, a painful divorce and the lonely life and hard work that follows. This can be accomplished by annihilating divorce and stopping it dead in its tracks.

I also want to equip you to heal from past issues, so that when you find yourself in the arms of your true love, they will have the sincere opportunity to get to know the real you and embrace a productive relationship with you. A relationship that could last forever; if you do not allow your pain or your past to hinder you from freely giving love another try.

So to each and every couple that is reading this book, may your lives and marriages become all that you've ever dreamed of. And to the single person that is in search of the relationship that you desire, be courageous. There is a mate out there waiting for you. And you can grow and develop now so that when they arrive you are ready for a blessed union. It takes courage to try love again, to give yourself and your heart to another person who is quite honestly, capable of letting you down. But we are all human, and we all have the capacity to fail and to succeed; to be right and to be wrong. And this is why it takes courage to grow and walk through life in the arms of another.

This book is filled with hope, joy, and laughter. It is also filled with tests and lessons. And it is my desire to see each and every one of you in a happy, loving and strong relationship. You are what the world is looking for. The Strongest Marriages in America.

1
The Greatest Gift

I believe that finding the person that you will spend the rest of your life with is a spectacular thing. Marriage is one of the greatest gifts known to man.

Think about it. You are born and raised by your parents or loved ones. And then you transition into adulthood. You are in a world of different ethnic groups that have a particular culture that they live by and people who have experienced life, love, religion and academics differently than you have. So we become adults, and our next stage or phase is building a new unit, a family. And we accomplish discovering and building that family in so many different ways.

We are all thrown into this gigantic pool of people throughout the earth in search of our future family. We

discover what we like and what we do not like as we date and one day we meet Mr. or Mrs. Tomorrow. Some people have parents who adhere to a culture that arranges marriages for them. Others have no clue what a relationship looks like because they did not see their parents in a healthy relationship, so they test drive love and crash until they find the right car. There are other people who have seen love displayed in their family and the son looks for someone like his mom in a woman, and the daughter looks for someone like her dad in a man. And all of that can happen to us consciously or subconsciously. There are so many different ways to find love and lifetime companionship that I cannot name them all, nevertheless, it is a journey.

When this journey ends, and we find Mr. or Mrs. Tomorrow, everything should change. We should feel safer, and we should have more stability. Marriage is supposed to be the answer to so many things in life for us. How beautiful and what a gracious a gift, not to have to spend your life alone. To have someone that you can build your future with, I mean actually, *architect* life with. To take someone's heart in to account and serve them with your love. To accept their flaws and celebrate their strengths.

Marriage is a gift that we can place no monetary value on, for it far exceeds monetary or numeric calculations. To love someone. To change because it is needed, not because you have to. To lovingly nudge

them in the right direction. To have someone else's best interest at heart. To give what you can never really take back, love.

When you dedicate your life to someone so many amazing things begin to happen. It is almost as if together you two become super heroes. You are the only one who knows your spouse the way you do. You know how they move and maneuver through life. You are the one who prays for each other and stands up for each other. The two of you evaluate and take on life's challenges together. You support each other and design a life together. So often people do not really value what is truly taking place when they get married. That marriage is special and powerful. And when handled properly, you will be blown away by how things fall in place. To share your life with the one you love, and someone who loves you is such a gift.

Marriage is a gift that is wrapped in the bow of life waiting for us to take a chance and give true love a try. So take hold of this gift and treasure it. Never forsaking it and always holding it in high regard. The value that you place on it will serve you well and in the end you will say that is was all worth it.

Tools Page

What Tools Have You Learned In This Chapter?

_____

_____

_____

_____

_____

_____

_____

_____

_____

_____

_____

_____

_____

_____

_____

_____

_____

_____

_____

_____

2
A Love System

The goal is to Establish Intimacy, Romance, and Happiness in Today's Marriages. One of the ways that can be done is by developing a Love System that works for you as a couple. Webster's dictionary defines love as a feeling of strong or constant affection for a person. I would like to focus on one word here, Constant. Constant is defined as staying the same, not changing and always loyal. So we could say that love is "the act of having a strong affection for a person that never changes." *So I must ask you.* When you tell your husband or wife (present or to be) that you love them, are you committed to never changing your emotional position concerning them regardless of their failures and human flaws? If you can say yes, then you have probably developed a foundation of friendship, not feelings.

Because feelings can change but true friendship never changes. I am not suggesting that everything will be perfect. Emotions are fluid. They will change. There will be things that challenge you and the relationship. But what I am saying is that your emotional "position" towards them does not change. So you may say, "I do not like how this is making me feel, but I am still with you in this." I am suggesting that when your relationship is challenged that this is someone that you are willing to fight with and fight for. That real love guides your decisions regarding each other.

Real love grants permission to the other party to affect or impact your life and the lives of those you love, and that love you. Both people have to make a decision to commit to the other one's life and commit to an unbreakable friendship. True friendship means that their journey and challenges as they develop, do not negate your role in their life, your commitment to them, or their commitment to you. Anyone can be in a relationship with someone but being their companion and partner in life is taking that relationship to another level.

As a companion and partner, you will experience their fears, growth, development and even their failures. All of those situations will and can positively and negatively affect you. That means that you trust them with your life, even in their weakness. True friendship means that you will pack your bags for the journey called life and ride every road with them. Friendship says that

you will buckle up and take the flight of life with them in blue skies or during thunder storms.

Friendship is important because romance can be situational. I am not saying that being attracted to your spouse is situational, though it can be for some. I am saying that situations can dictate when and if you are able to express or act on that attraction, so attraction is probably not what you want to build your relationship on. For instance, you may be spending time with your family, one of you may not be feeling well, or you may be separated because of your work schedule or other various reasons. During those times romance and intimacy will not be possible, but your friendship will travel the miles of life with you. So, if you depend on the attraction between the two of you to give your relationship longevity, I can guarantee you that at some point one of you will be disappointed.

Having an attraction is very important, and we will focus on that later in the book, but it is very unlikely that it will preserve the life of the relationship on its own.

Friendship is also important because each

person is going to change. We all change. We mature and grow older, we become wiser and at some point we have a clearer view of who we are and who we are not. We aspire to achieve one goal or dream during some period of our life but as time goes on and things progress our aspirations may change. These changes are not always synchronized. Sometimes one of us grows faster than the other. The key is working with each other through each change instead of fighting each other through the transition. It is important not to depend on how you feel in any of these instances to maintain this relationship but depend on the common thread of companionship, trust, and commitment to seal your love.

The changes will also reveal if you are truly happy. Someone may say to you that the person you are dating makes you so happy. They have no idea that they make you laugh, but they do not make you happy. There is a distinct difference between someone who makes things exciting and fun and someone who puts you first and truly desires to make you happy. They can tell the best jokes and still drain you emotionally. Which of course means that they do not make you happy. Happiness is when you both are completely open with each other, and it is okay. They do not care about your temper tantrums, and you do not care about them pouting. You are happy with them just the way they are. You can tolerate their flaws without feeling overwhelmed or drained. And you enjoy their presence in your life. You might even say that

you do not know what you would do without them. Now, that's happy. It is when you can let your hair down, and feel comfortable saying "Hey, this is me,' and know that they will not judge you but continue to strive to make you happy. I believe that you can have this type of happiness.

Let's Put It Into Action

Now let's talk about your personal Love System. A system is defined as any formulated, regular, or special method or plan of procedure. ***So here is your second question.*** What plan will the two of you put in place to accommodate and support the love and friendship that you profess for each other? We have all heard the old adage, "If you fail to plan, you plan to fail." This system or plan is not really something I or anyone else can give you. It is something that the two of you will develop from the information and tools that you read in this book and from all of the information that you will gather from everything that is around you. You will find a form at the end of this chapter to help you prioritize your target areas and develop a plan together that both of you can live with. Remember to add a timeline even if it is only to revisit how the plan for that target area is working. The great thing about all of this is that you two have the opportunity to come up with the plan together, and you can always tweak it. My advice to you is to remain

flexible, be honest and remain true to how you personally feel. Whenever you sacrifice how you personally feel you are in danger of one day resenting the other person for a sacrifice that they do not even realize you are making for them. They have no idea that you are quietly suffering because you are afraid of verbalizing how you personally feel.

The reason that some people refrain from verbalizing how they feel is because they think the other person may not be vested enough to work through the issue they have and/or break up with them. Others may feel like the relationship will not survive the true observation of how they view the other person's issues.

In short, they want the relationship more than they want, to be honest. So they just shrug off when the other person says or does something that conflicts with how they feel, what they need or what they want. The problem with that is one day it is *ALL* going to come out. Everything runs over when it's full. Beware the art of silently suffering. In most cases, you are simply prolonging the inevitable. If they are not committed, they are not committed. If they are committed, they are committed. You should know where they really stand concerning you and the direction you are going in early on in the relationship. Once you have confirmed that they are committed, it is full steam ahead.

A great way to make sure that both of your needs are met is by actively working to fulfill your mate's needs.

And the only way to be sure that happens is for both of you to be clear about what those needs are. Out love each other. It is almost like a contest. If the both of you focus on each other's needs, then no one feels deprived or taken advantage of. That information will be very important as you develop your Love System or Relationship Plan.

Let me give you a few examples of identifying the things that are important to both of you and developing a plan around those topics.

One of the target areas that you want to develop a strategy for and include in your plan is communication. Why? Because **communication** helps to form alliances, partnerships and develops families. Partnerships yield results which is why it is so important to take heed to who you communicate with the most. Communication causes you to fall in love in your personal life, and it causes you to build successful companies in your professional life. Communication is to a relationship like air is to the body; you will surely die without it and so will a relationship. Men and women vary differently in this area. Some men talk to you initially to get to know more about you and your family. Once they have enough information they can make a decision about marrying you. Once they give you their last name they have had the last of what they feel like are the deep, revealing, and in-depth conversations between the two of you, because they have the information that they need. But the woman

thought that you were talking to her because you were building a bond and it was establishing intimacy between you. That intimacy caused her to be more aroused and attracted to you. It made her feel connected to you. When you stopped talking to her or denied her access to converse with you, your actions told her that you no longer felt the same way, when all along you simply needed to clarify in your love plan how you both communicate. You have to find a medium because Charles is waiting for her at work and he cannot wait to talk to her all day long.

Words are like love to a woman. They mean everything. They say a father's words affirm and establish a woman's identity. If that is the case, can you imagine what the words from the man she is intimate with does for her? **Everything!** To the contrary, the lack of words can be devastating for her. He thinks she has become difficult because she is snappy and irritable when all along it was because he didn't feel the need to talk to her or listen to her. Now the same holds true for women. When they feel rejected or betrayed by this man who they believe is failing to communicate with them, they say all of the WRONG things. What is so interesting about that is they really do not mean it, if they did they would have left already. They just want him to do what he did to get them in the first place. They feel like he misled them. He showed her one kind of relationship in the beginning, and then he switched gears after she

became vested only to check out on her, or so she thinks. She is not happy, and all he hears from her is, she is not happy. If no one stops this cycle and says to the other one "What do you need from me?" that relationship is over. Most of the time each one says what "they" need. He says he needs to handle some things alone, and she says I need you to talk to me. Rarely does one of them have enough trust in the other person to focus on the other ones need. They do not trust that they will get the same in return or that their mate is going to make a decision that will show them that they are a priority. They fear that if they do not look out for themselves, they will never be loved the way they desire. And most of the time, people do not make the decision in favor of their mate's needs. They selfishly take care of themselves with no regard for how the other person feels or is impacted. Now, two people who really loved each other have to start all over with someone else because no one said, "I will try to give you what you need." Instead, they verbalize what they want. They failed to communicate properly.

That is why the lack of communication is so dangerous. People and countries can start wars, cause harm and damage lives when they lack in or fail to communicate; especially when they fail to communicate with integrity and properly. Communication solidifies unions, and the lack of it destroys commitments. This is important for both of you to understand because who you

talk to the most is who you have the strongest partnership or alliances with. That means that even though it is important to have healthy relationships with others, your primary relationship, and your most impactful communication should be with your spouse or your spouse to be. Even though no one can live your life for you, they can support you better and assist you more appropriately in life if the communication is clear and consistent.

Another area that you might want to include is how you can take care of yourself without the other person misunderstanding your need to do so. Everyone needs **"ME TIME"**. There is no getting around it. Some of us may need more or less than others, but everyone needs it. For instance, some people find a room in the house and stay in that room for hours. It could be the restroom, the man cave, the video game room, the kitchen, the patio; wherever it is, they sit there for hours. Sometimes doing nothing and other times doing everything. It's like their safe and protected place. Their place of solitude. What you will hear over a period of time from the other person is "You know where he is. In his man cave where he always is." Now, the truth is that he is only there a few hours a day. But his wife will say he is always there because she doesn't understand the need for that space and his need for personal me time. *And we compete or have concerns with anything we do not understand.* So now, she makes him choose between her and his safe

haven. A word of advice, even he chooses you physically and leaves his man cave; mentally he is still there. He is probably just attempting to keep the peace. The same is true for a woman who loves her study, sunroom or kitchen.

What would resolve all of this is having the process or target area of taking care of yourself in your plan. Each person would have clarity about what the other person's personal needs were. They would not feel rejected or disappointed because they would realize that it is not personal or a form of rejection. If someone has dealt with rejection in their life before, their experience might cause them to misjudge their spouses need in this area. So again, communicating your weakness or scars from the past is important. And when you come together to discuss a target area like this it is important for both of you to be understanding and honest. Remember at the beginning of the book we talked about how people grew up or were raised differently, which means everyone is exposed to different experiences in their family life. Well, this would be one of the places that this might apply, so keep that in mind. They may have grown up in a loud, rowdy home, and you may have had a simple, quiet home.

Since life could have been displayed so different for each of you, I encourage you to list the things that are important to you and develop a plan around that list. As you grow and your lives change so will your list. One of

the keys to longevity will be updating your plan when necessary and proactively. When you identify that something is getting off track, address it as soon as time permits. After you develop your relationship rhythm, this process will become much easier. If you implement what you have read here about love and having a system for your relationship, together you will see a relationship evolve that will take you beyond any happiness that you could have ever imagined.

Nothing can defeat a made up mind. So if the two of you make up your mind that this relationship is what you want, then everything around you has to line up with that confession. Your love and partnership will defy the odds and overcome challenges that cripple and destroy other couples. Marriages can survive turbulent storms and even be repaired. The key is your willingness and commitment to have a marriage that stands the test of time. To have or become what we call, "One of the Strongest Marriages in America."

Love System

This form can be used to develop your Love Plan/System. Remember that this is a working plan and should be revised as needed.

1. Target Area

2. Plan

3. Timeline

Love System

This form can be used to develop your Love Plan/System. Remember that this is a working plan and should be revised as needed.

1. Target Area

_____
_____
_____
_____
_____

2. Plan

_____
_____
_____
_____
_____
_____
_____
_____
_____

3. Timeline

_____
_____

Love System

This form can be used to develop your Love Plan/System. Remember that this is a working plan and should be revised as needed.

1. Target Area

2. Plan

3. Timeline

Love System

This form can be used to develop your Love Plan/System. Remember that this is a working plan and should be revised as needed.

1. Target Area

2. Plan

3. Timeline

3
Single Minded - Mindset

For a married couple, the Single Minded Mindset can ruin a marriage. I cannot tell you how many couples never really think or talk about the transition process that comes with moving in together. It can be a time when both people discover how selfish or controlling the other person can be. They love each other, and they cannot wait to live together, but they do not always take into account what that process is really like. The two individual lives become one. And if you can master a middle ground on the things that are needed to blend your lives together, you will minimize unnecessary arguments. The key is to welcome the addition instead of fearing the loss. You do not lose your privacy; you gain a partner, a person that is concerned about your well-being. You are not merely giving up

space in your closet or your right to make decisions on your own; you gain a sounding board and someone to help balance your emotions. It is a very interesting space when you go from having the freedom to do whatever you want, to having to incorporate a system that enables two people to cohabitate. But there are some things that you can discuss while you are getting to know each other that will make the transition smoother, when and if you decide to get married because you will already know the nuances.

For example: You can address these questions in your readers guide.

1. Where are you spiritually?
2. How you pay your bills? Online, due date, etc.
3. Synchronizing or the blending of your sleeping habits. Are you a night owl or an early bird?
4. The way or how often you clean?
5. How you do your laundry or keep your closet?
6. How you handle children, if either of you has any?
7. How you cook or what you eat? No Pork, Vegan, etc.
8. How do you deal with your family and friends?
9. What you do at and after work? Exercise, quiet time at home, etc.

10. The time and money that you spend on extracurricular activities? Do you have a budget for this?

11. Intimacy? A little, a lot, enjoy, etc.

These are just a few things to consider so you will be prepared to compromise with each other and build a life together. You may have to take some time to process what you discover, but you can do it. You can find a way to combine your lives and not feel like you are giving up everything. You are so much stronger together and over time when the moving dust settles, you will welcome the change and the addition to your life.

On the other hand, if you are not married and have begun to think about marriage this information might also work in your favor. You can go ahead and start making the adjustments that you need to now in order to incorporate someone else into your life. Take a personal inventory and look at how well organized you are. Do you have room for someone else in your life? Will their life fit into yours and vice versa? If not, take the steps and make the minor adjustments necessary to accomplish just that. And it should be a win, win for both of you. We all have to give up something; (that favorite couch or picture) but you gain so much more than what you are giving up. Take a deep breath, look around your life at what really matters and put a plan in place so you will be prepared for the relationship that you long for.

When we have not truly addressed some of these areas, or we fail to be honest with ourselves, and our mate things can take a turn for the worst. One of the reasons why I believe we are not able to maintain a healthy marriage is because of what I have defined as relationship immaturity. You have to be a mature individual to take into account someone else's feelings, needs, and even their expectations.

Author and Christian Leader, Ricardo Dorcean shares as it pertains to relationships, that when men shut down, they haven't matured enough to allow someone in their personal and emotional space. The outcome, when this issue arises can be disappointing. The failure to be able to adequately resolve issues is primarily because of his own unresolved issues or the lack of maturity. That immaturity causes men to shut people out in an effort to handle things on their own while failing to understand the impact that can have on someone who loves them and considers you to be a part of each other's lives. Some other reasons that men shut down might be because we feel guilty about our mistakes, we assume that what we have done is beyond repair, or that we are the reason it broke down in the first place. And even with that rational, the reality is that is still an issue of immaturity. Now there are also times where a man may feel justified for shutting down, for instance; if a man feels disrespected he will disengage, even if it is a result of something he did. That is a manhood defense

mechanism. But that still exposes his immaturity because he hasn't learned how to simply confront and resolve the issue without being consumed by it.

Just like some men fail to handle things properly, so do some women. Women find themselves emotionally and verbally responding in a manner that is not normally their communication style. They go from being loving and supportive to angry and verbally offensive. Most of the time that is because the type of behavior they see demonstrated by the man they love resembles and stings like rejection. And the truth is that neither men nor women like to be or feel rejected, especially when they think that they are in a relationship with someone. The difference is most of the time women will talk it out and men will not. As men, we need to learn how to deal with confrontation, deal with our differences and even the things that may be said in an argument when we have hurt someone; without shutting down. Maybe shutting down is the process that your man has utilized all of his life so that he is not wounded or hurt in a relationship. But he can find a way, like using some of the tools in this book to help deescalate the argument and not respond to the fear of being damaged by it or shut down. If he wants to truly be loved, he has to become better at talking things out and resolving the problems at hand, because if he does not he will see this in all of his relationships since every woman he dates will be human. And at some point, her feelings may get hurt, and this may be how she

responds. One thing is for sure, shutting down is never the answer and most of the time, it will do more harm than taking the time to talk things out. It is time for all of us, men and women to do a better job and grow up if we want our relationships to last.

I agree with that observation. I also believe that sometimes we can even be a little selfish instead of selfless. We are by nature a bit possessive and maybe selfish over what life grants us. Just think about a two-year-old child who has never been taught to lie, steal or be selfish. If you put them in a room with other children, and they find a toy that they like, they will hold on to the toy, and when asked to share the toy they will say "mine" as they grasp it closely to their chest with their eyes filled with tears. This child feels like this item belongs to them because they like it. They do not think about who purchased it, who it actually belongs to or if someone else is fond of the toy as well. All they know is that they want it to be theirs. As this child matures over time, he or she begins to understand what sharing means and most of the time they develop into well-rounded logical young adults. The same thing is sometimes true in relationships.

Even though we meet someone else that we fall in love with, when we think about the relationship we are thinking about how (we) feel about the relationship. That it makes (us) happy, that it is something that (we) want or that (we) have a strong attraction for the person. Very

42

seldom will you find someone who has just met someone, and they say "You know, I want to make them happy, so I should probably marry them. I am going to sacrifice my life and my resources to give them the best life possible." No, we are like the two-year-old. We see something we like, and we grab it and hold it close to our chest, and we say "mine." That kind of desire to please the other person typically happens after they have fallen in love. And even then it is a growing process. We generally do not start off thinking about giving them what they need. We start off believing that they satisfy a need in us. And you may not even consciously be aware of this.

I hope that this book will cause us to grow just like the two-year-old; into someone that operates in relationship maturity. Taking into account how another person feels, how they are impacted by us and having their best interest at heart. I am not by any stretch of the imagination implying that you should not regard yourself at all. But what I am saying is that if you make a sincere effort to operate according to your own desires and to meet the needs of the person that you love, I believe you will experience a win-win. If you focus on the other person's needs and they focus on your needs then both of you will be able to give each other what you need. But if both of you are always focusing on your own needs you will constantly struggle because you're only in a relationship with yourself, not the other person. A

relationship is about what you can give; it is about how you can love. When it is only about what you can get, then there are going to be some major challenges.

4
I'm So Tired of Being Single

You have probably said this or heard someone else say it. Maybe you experienced a bad break up, or maybe you have not dated in a long time, and you feel like it is never going to happen. Maybe you are lonely and tired of eating dinner alone. We all know that loneliness can be an emotional monster for men or women. *Attention* – babies cry for it and men die for it. All of these things can make you say, "I am so tired of being single." Regardless of how you arrived at this emotion, it's awful. You go to events alone. It seems like everywhere you go there are only couples there and that you are always the third wheel. There is no one to share your goals, desires, joys, problems, dreams or financial responsibilities with. And you are so tired of being single and doing it all alone. It sounds like gloom and doom

right? I am sure it does. But what I would like to talk to you about is your perspective.

Your perspective impacts how you view everything. Let me share with you the true definition of single and let's see if I can help you with your perspective. The definition of single is (of a person) not otherwise occupied; free to do something, or not currently involved in a sexual or romantic relationship.

If we take a close look at the definition, it does not look like gloom and doom. It looks like a person that is available for an opportunity. It says that the person is free to do something. You are free to follow your dreams without restriction until your spouse shows up. You have no limits on how much time you spend furthering your education. You have no limits on the time or resources that you spend on developing yourself or improving your life. You are available for all of the opportunity in the world, with no restrictions. For perspective sake, I would like you to take this time to fine tune your life, from improving your credit score to making sure that you are in the best physical shape possible. Consider this as a time of preparation versus a time of loneliness or rejection. This is the time for you to discover yourself. How you want to look or dress. What interest you want to pursue and places that you would like to visit. Who knows, your spouse may find you while you are on this

adventure to fine tune yourself.

Changing your perspective about being single will take the pressure off of dating. People pick up on your signals and your behavior. The last thing you want to do is appear lonely and desperate. One of my mentors, Dr. Jewel Diamond Taylor says that "Desperation is a terrible perfume to wear." So you want to exhibit an attitude or posture of confidence. You are the only one who can change your perspective about what single looks and feels like to you. And if you change your perspective you can avoid that stigma. This new perspective will display you as secure and confident. It will make for great conversation and get rid of the pressure some people experience while dating. And let's be honest. Dating in this day and age can already be horrific. We need to focus on who we are encountering more than we focus on how lonely we are. Let's spend our energy on evaluating if this is the best person for you, not on how badly we want to be in a relationship.

The truth is that you are the best YOU that was ever born. There is no one else out there or in this world like you. You are an original. There is someone out there that will appreciate a secure, confident and loving you. Decide how you want to look and exactly what you want to be. Work hard to accomplish your goals and everything else will fall into place. Focus on yourself while you have the time to because ALL of that will change when the love of your life finds you. My advice,

enjoy your single life while you can; having done all that you want to do so when love comes, you can enjoy your marriage too.

5
The Dynamics of Divorce

arriage is one of the most incredible life-changing experiences that you could ever have. It alters the course of your life, and it collides you with another person with whom you craft a future. Your life seems to take on a new sense of purpose, and you find great joy in the arms of the one you love. To the contrary, divorce can be devastating to not only the couple but to the children and the extended family. It can cause financial hardship, emotional damage, and immeasurable stress. It is amazing that two things that are the polar opposite of each other are so radically intertwined. It is with that understanding that we enter into the sanctity of holy matrimony. We wed with the hopes that the person that is standing across from us, ready to place the ring on our finger is fully

committed to us for the rest of our life. We understand that divorce could be a possible option based on the direction of the relationship. But it is our hope that it is not a route that we will ever have to take or encounter. It is our hope that we not only receive a mate but a life's partner that will weather the vicissitudes of life with us.

It is important to understand that marriage is 50/50. It is a give and take. There will be times when you give more, or you take more, but the goal is to balance out the two. I hope that as you are reading, you find the tools that will assist you in maneuvering through the unity of marriage and the pitfalls of divorce. These tools will help you as you engage in the necessary process of building a strong, healthy and lasting relationship. Remember, the goal is to annihilate divorce. To stop it dead in its tracks and maintain the marriages that started out with such glee. It is also to establish a common ground so that both parties involved can actively participate in the design and structure of a marriage that will last.

If properly utilized and committed to, this information could help a couple transform where they currently are into an oasis of love. If you are currently married and looking for a way or a plan to rescue your relationship, stop at the end of each chapter and have a real conversation with the understanding that you really want your marriage to work regardless of what you need to confess or share now.

This is important for me to state because I know that my ex-husband and I failed to take these measures. I personally feel like anyone can resolve marital issues if they sincerely want to, and I DO NOT want you to end up divorced. I am waging a war against divorce from two different aspects. First by addressing the dynamics of divorce and the strain and stress that follow. So often couples dissolve their marriages over something that does not even compare to the challenges that they will face once they become divorced and alone. One of the things that I have found to be extremely successful is getting a couple to map out what their lives will look like after divorce and if maybe, just maybe, it might wiser to work on their issues instead of ending their marriage.

Secondly by preparing individuals prior to getting married, so that they can have a better chance at building a successful marriage. It is my goal to help them avoid problems that are encountered when ill prepared thus guiding them in selecting the appropriate spouse and avoiding the divorce altogether. Some of the ways to equip someone for marriage is to ensure that they have a clear understanding of what it takes to have a successful marriage and the work that goes into it.

This is important because divorce has become extremely casual. Some people take the easy way out only to find themselves divorced again because they did not possess the proper tools the first time. That is why I

am so driven about sharing the information in this book. The strategy is twofold: to educate and equip the married couple and the single person so that they make better decisions, have better judgment and are skilled enough to maneuver properly through the intricate waters of relationships.

I share this with the hopes of preserving someone's marriage. I have either witnessed and or experienced the pitfalls of divorce myself, and I do not wish that reality on anyone. The culprits of divorce do not take any mercy on a couple or family. They creep into a marriage and try relentlessly to end it. You know the top 10 culprits of divorce. You have probably seen these culprits in someone else's relationship. Or maybe you are like me, and you have had the first-hand experience of the issues they inflict on a marriage. These culprits can cause feelings of heartbreak, disappointment and even possibly rage.

Those top 10 culprits are money, sex, work, affairs, miscommunication, blended families, in-laws, the Ex, illness, and pride. These are not the only culprits that facilitate successful divorces, but they are some of the ones that have a profound impact.

It is with a heavy heart that I penned these pages. But I am determined and armed with the sincere hope that my burning desire to annihilate divorce in America would by some small measure, help someone save their

own marriage. I believe that if two people really commit to each other and work together, anything is possible. I hope that with the information that I share and the things that you read, you will humble yourself to each other and commit to building a marriage worth having. We do not want to make marriage any more complicated than it has to be.

Life is already complicated. As a successful woman in corporate American and later as an entrepreneur, I am sure that it appeared as if I had it all together and that life was all good. But the truth is, though my needs were met and I continued to build my business, doing it alone was not my ideal plan or goal. It is extremely hard and exhausting when you are sitting alone in an emergency room at 2:00 AM with a sick and crying one year old in one arm and a sleepy four year old in the other. Now that they are both in High School, I look back with immense gratitude because we made it. But at the time, it seemed like it was never going to end. People encounter these obstacles all of the time because they have to, but I am sure if they had someone to share that burden with, it would make things so much easier.

Those are the little things that go unspoken when you consent to divorce. Paying and budgeting all the bills alone. Purchasing a home or buying a car alone. Raising and developing children alone. Not to mention having someone who knows and loves you. Not just someone

that you are with and/or like to hang out with but someone who knows your good, your bad and your ugly and they are okay with who you truly are. That is what matters and that is what truly makes the difference, having a secure partner in life and in true love that you can depend on.

As strong as we are as individuals it can still be a source of comfort or relief to be able to partner with someone that you can win with. There are really no words to articulate what it's like to have to deal with family life alone. Women and men alike do it all of the time, and I am sure we can, for the most part, both agree that it is not the ideal situation to be in. First of all, raising a family alone is not how a family was designed to operate. It was designed to be a structured and nurturing unit according to God's plan. There is order to the dynamics that produce a healthy family unit. And so when you are trying to raise a family alone, there's a missing component from what was designed to be carried out and operated by two people. So when there is only one person trying to maintain two roles it can cause extreme pressure and even failure in some areas.

I believe that I would have made different decisions concerning marriage if I knew the true impact of divorce prior to getting married or if I had been more informed in our failed counseling sessions that ultimately led to divorce. I am almost positive that I would have done a

lot of things differently. I have to be honest and say that I may not have even of married him in the first place if I knew then what I know now. Not that he wasn't a good person, per say. We just had extremely different views of what love and fidelity look like. Fidelity is faithfulness to a person, cause, or belief, demonstrated by continuing loyalty and support. Because of how I grew up, I needed that. But that's not how he grew up. His father had children out of wedlock, and his mother was able to handle that. His mother handling it looked like love to him. The fact that I did not tolerate any infidelity looked like I didn't love him, to him. And the opposite was true for me. Not putting me in that position would have looked like love to me. Placing me in that position was far from what I thought love looked like.

That is why you want to know someone's past and how they view relationships, love, and commitment. Be clear about what they believe and desire from you. Know what standard they hold themselves to if any and express your standards. We are often disappointed when we have an expectation that is not met. Expectation is the mother of our frustration. We expect something or a particular behavior from our mate, and when they fail us, disappointment sets in and the problems follow. That is why we need to express our expectation with a sincere heart and try to have a clear understanding of each other. Clarity is key when you are giving someone else the

reigns to your life. Be clear and hear what is said to you with both ears.

These things are important because marriage is full of pitfalls. My hope is to be able to articulate these pitfalls that can lead to divorce and give you the necessary information to avoid divorce. It is my goal to demonstrate the appropriate solutions to alleviate stress, fear and disappointment and in doing so, promote unity and success in marriage.

6
Sacred Partnership

Marriage is one of the most strategic and important partnerships that you will ever engage in. It is sacred. It is consist of two people and only two people. It is legally binding, and truth be told regardless of what is sometimes depicted in our society, marriage is also spiritually binding. Marriage can positively or negatively affect your financial standing and so many other aspects of your life.

A partner is defined as a relationship resembling a legal partnership and usually involving close cooperation between parties, having specified and joint rights and responsibilities. You read that correctly. **Joint rights and responsibilities.** You can scream all day

about your **rights**, just make sure you are screaming just a loud and be just as vocal about your **responsibility**. You have a responsibility to each other, your children and your extended family. That is something that leads back to relationship maturity. When people are mature, they take responsibility for their actions and their decisions. They understand that they cannot take what they want and not give what they have. Do not in your actions, deeds or decisions take that responsibility lightly. You two are in this relationship together. And it is important that your commitment to each other is reflected in what you say and in what you do.

Pilot and Co-pilot

Since you are in this together, let's find a way to put some clarity to what you are reading. Relationships are like airplanes. When you decide that you want to be married to someone, you need to ask yourself if you want to be this persons co-pilot as a woman. As a man, you want to ask yourself if you want this person to be your co-pilot and if you are willing to take responsibility for being their pilot? This is important because no one can get off of a plane when it is in flight. Marriage means that you are in flight. *NOONE IS GETTING OFF. (I have to pause here and tell you that I think I am a comedian, and I am laughing so hard right now.)* If being a pilot

and a co-pilot on a flight that no one was able to get off of was communicated in marriage counseling, I wonder how many people would go through with it.

Let's move on. Every airplane that leaves the runway has the possibility of crashing. Now, they all have what is called a flight path. That path can be determined by several things. The most direct route between two points is known as the "Great Circle" line that connects the two points. Flights will often deviate from the Great Circle routing for a variety of reasons.

- First, is air traffic congestion; air traffic control can route planes through different corridors if others have too many planes already in them.
- Second, is wind/weather. If the headwinds are too strong, then it often becomes faster to fly a more southerly route that is longer distance wise. In the case of a massive storm along the Great Circle path, the plane will also deviate from the shortest route.
- Third, a plane will not fly the Great Circle route if there are no suitable diversion airports along the flight path.

Some of these are hard to predict but on the other hand, there are some things about planes that we do know. We know where they are taking off from and where they are supposed to land. We know who is

supposed to be flying them and what time they are scheduled to arrive and are scheduled to depart. But at a moment's notice, the plane could hit turbulence or enter into a storm of some sort. Hopefully, the plane will recover. But what happens if the plane does not recover? The plane crashes.

Relationships are the same way. Love and planning cannot always avoid a storm or turbulence. Anything can happen. And you have to know that the person you now share your last name with is up for anything. How can that be achieved? How can two people know, as much as possible if they have found Mr. or Mrs. Anything?

First, both people have to decide who they want to be, and that is not for the other party to do for them. They have to have a personal conviction about what they stand for, represent or allow in their life. You cannot control or mold the other person. You can support their growth and process but at the end of the day, they are the only ones who can determine and commit to becoming a loving, unselfish person and operate with good character and integrity towards you and others. We all have the freedom to make decisions, positively or negatively; good or bad because we are still our own person even after we marry someone.

The challenge is deciding what kind of man or woman you want to be and once you make that decision, can you live with it? Can you look at yourself and like

what you see? Who do you choose to be for yourself, your family and your spouse? If all was revealed about who you really are, would you be proud of who that person is? You want to be conscious that you are in a relationship. Be aware that there are two people flying the plane, and if you have children, then you have passengers. And one of the things that you always want to ask yourself when you are making decisions is, if what you are going to do is going to cause the plane to crash.

Secondly, both people have to be ready. You have to meet people at a time when they are ready. You can be attracted to and get along well with someone who is not ready. They could have debt that haunts them, be focused on their career, they could still have feelings for someone else even though it is over or they could be grieving a loved one that they have lost. How about this. They could just like their life just like it is and it is not the time for them to shift yet. When you commit to someone who is not committed to you, and they are simply not ready, you do both of you an injustice. It is okay to ask them, are you ready for a committed relationship with the goal being marriage. And give them the comfort of knowing that they can be honest.

One of the reasons that the other person may not be honest is because they like you and want to spend time with you. You are good for them, and they do not want to lose that. But the simple term for that is selfishness. If

they know that you want two different things, and they lead you on to believe they want what you want just to keep you around, that is plain old selfishness. My grandfather would have said that "they cannot have their cake and eat it too," which is an ancient proverb that literally means "you cannot simultaneously retain your cake and eat it." Once the cake is eaten, it is gone. That is not what love is anyway. That is being dishonest, and it happens all of the time. Love is honest, and love gives you a choice, not a trap.

Having to have these "Adult Conversations" are not fun at all. Believe me when I tell you, I know that. I am currently back on the dating scene, and boy let me tell you, it is something out here. You find someone or are found by someone that you really care for, and now you have to go and ruin it by being an adult. But be the adult you must, if you want to really enjoy a healthy marriage. It is okay to have fun and enjoy the blooming relationship but when it comes to the things that will establish or destroy the foundation of our union, "Someone has to be the adult in this relationship." (I told you that I thought I was hilarious.)

These conversations can save you so much time and heartache. If you continually see signs that you are a convenience or that you are not their priority, take heed to those signs. Watch what they do, you cannot always believe what they say. Actions denote importance or

priority. People will bust a move (take care of something promptly) when something is important to them. And another thing, if you have to have these conversations a few times that's a sign for you to duck and run. Their heart is not in it, or there is something else going on in their life. Either way, run for the hills.

Now, even if they are misleading it is up to us to determine how far we will allow them to operate in our lives and ultimately they are not going to break off the relationship. You have to do that. This person has no intention of committing. They are not ready but they like you and what you have to offer. It is not fair for someone to ask you to commit to them when they have no intention of honoring the relationship or marriage. Their only intention is to operate in it long enough to get what's in it for them. If they honored it, that would mean that they respect it and hold it in high regard. If that were the case or on their mind, we would not be having this author – reader conversation. You would know where they really stand. Listen, no one has any time to waste. Who wants to give someone years of their life and that person never planned on staying in the first place? A great question to ask yourself is, "What's in it for me too?" If you cannot list at least five things, run and run as fast as you can. You do not want to live your life with someone that only takes from you and never adds anything to you. They are constantly making

withdrawals but never making any deposits. This Is The Rest Of Your Life!

Next, ask each other this question. "Why are the two of you together?" What does he want? Love, intimacy, a hot meal, a clean home, help in business or ministry or companionship? What does she want? Provision, support, understanding, comfort, compassion or sensitivity? Now, these are merely suggestions. I know that everyone wants something different. Make sure you know what your mate needs and wants. And then the other person can honestly express whether or not they can commit to that need or want.

You see, one of the reasons that people fail in relationships is because they are unclear about the cost or the investment. They think that what they experienced while they 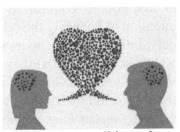 were dating is all there is but we are talking about someone's life becoming your life. That means that it includes their deepest hurts, fears and maybe even their unique desires. (Yes, I said unique.) You both need to know what you have to give and what you are going to receive.

The clarity in that will help you make some decisions and communicate authentically with each other.

7
Getting to Know Your Mate

About 15 years ago I was at a business training and one of the gentleman speaking taught on personality types using animals. There are so many of these personality and characteristic test available now that you can have your pick to choose from based on how you process information. I've tried to find where I originally heard this, but you can search the internet and see that it is everywhere, but I wasn't able to find where I originally took the training. Animals were catchy to me, so I am going to use them in my examples.

My understanding is this. We are born with personality traits. These traits are innate, inherent and natural; these traits are in us. Character traits or behavior are learned and can be molded, changed and developed

This information is important because if you can properly tell the difference between personality vs. character, then you will have a better idea about how the person that you are involved in a relationship with will progress; or not. This should also increase the quality of your understanding and communication with them. There is an old ancient script that says, "Wisdom is the principal thing; Therefore get wisdom. In all your getting, get understanding." When you make a decision to add someone to your life, to grant them access to your darkest secrets and most the vulnerable aspects of your life; you might want to understand who you are dealing with.

I am from North Carolina and being from the south there were certain expectations that your family had for a young man who was interested in dating you. There were just certain things that could not happen and if they did you better bet it was dealt with.

A. A young man could not blow his horn for one of us to come out of the house. He had to come to the door like a gentleman and ring the doorbell. (Our grandfather (Buddy, Buddy) would have a fit if that happened.)

B. A man did not use coarse language or strong language around women or children. They always waited for the women and children to leave and then they had their fun or had a drink if they wanted to.

C. A man opened the door for a young lady.

D. A man should not put his hands on a lady.

E. A man asked a lady's family for her hand in marriage and committed his loyalty to her.

F. If a man failed or an issue arose, he did not have to deal solely with his wife but her entire family. And that was okay because they entrusted her to his care.

G. And one of my favorite questions that Buddy, Buddy would ask our young suitors was, "Who are your people?" I know that sounds country but country he was, God rest his soul. I wish you could see the smile on my face right now. Basically, everything that he needed to know about you was in your bloodline. If your father was unfaithful or your mother was unladylike, he was not having it. Whew, that is funny to me now. We did not like it when he was grilling our little boyfriends, especially if we liked them. Oh, but how we appreciate our elders once we understand their rational.

Let me tell you that I miss those days. For the most part, a man of good character today has the wherewithal to still operate that way with his wife and family. But society has changed in the way people speak to and consider each other. The standard for social propriety has diminished. And it is starting early in our children with the music of today, there over exposure through the internet and television and the children they are exposed to in school. It is like we have lost an entire era of social

training. We no longer allow anyone to hold us accountable, and that has led to a decline in the propriety, appropriateness and the conventionally accepted standards of behavior or morals that we see today.

That is why I believe that it is so important for us to have a clear understanding of who someone really is; which is their *"personality"* and what that person is willing to become, which is their *"character."* After all, this is until death do you part. Not until you get fed up or feel defeated in your marriage. This is the DNA that will be deposited into your children and the DNA you will have to raise and nurture. This is part of the force that will govern your life and how it may possibly turn out. This is not simply great sex (or not so much) and a hearty laugh. This is your life we are talking about. With that being said, get a clear understanding of what and who you are committed to. There are questions you should be able to answer if your grandfather asks you who they are. Before you say, I Do you should at least be able to say yes to the following.

1. Will they protect your union at all cost?
2. Will they parent your children appropriately?
3. Will they work with you as you both transition and develop?
4. Will they partner with you in your finances?
5. Will they pray for you?
6. Will they fight for you?

7. Will they love you as you win and as you fail?

The answers to these questions are important and will help you gain a sense of security in your marriage. When you cook anything you need to know the ingredients and if you leave something out it does not turn out like the recipe said it would. That applies here also. Let's say that the personality traits are the ingredients and the character traits are the instructions. What are you baking? And how do you think it is going to turn out based on what you now know?

Take a good look at this for yourself. For instance, if there is a character flaw that they are willing to work on, chances are they will be able to do so. But if a personality trait is an issue, that might be a bit harder to resolve than you think, so try to be fair to the relationship by being honest about what you  see, not what they say. Properly evaluating what you are dealing with will allow you to make better decisions as far as a long term commitment is concerned and can help you bake a better cake.

4 Personality Types

I hope that after you read these descriptions, you will not only see your mate, but you will see yourself as well. Maybe by understanding these personalities it will help you understand how your loved one operates.

The four personality types that I would like to share with you are the Urchin, the Whale, the Shark, and the Dolphin. You will see similarities in each of these, but you will also see some extreme differences. Some people possess a little of all four of these types and others only possess one or two. I hope you can use this gauge to

determine where you and your mate fall in the list of personality types.

Urchin

Urchins are very analytical, cautious and sometimes they can be viewed as being a bit skeptical. Some say that they are somewhat conservative in their practices as well. You probably will not find them taking a lot of risks; they do not mind spending time alone, and they do not have the need to be a social butterfly. It is very easy to develop a relationship with them once you understand their personality style and realize that the fact that they may seem like an introvert is not an indication that they dislike you. They just aren't the friendliest personality type. And you will probably be surprised at how quickly the relationship bond develops between you two because once they connect with you, you never have to worry about where they stand. If they are in, they are in.

Urchins want to know the facts. They want to know the "5 W's":

Who? What? **When**? **Where**? **Why**? **How**?

You know these types of people. They want to know what needs to be done. When it needs to be complete. Who is doing what and what you need from them. You have to love them. All of the bases will be covered, and they are not going to let you down because they can't. It just is not in them not to complete a task, and they will

probably help you complete your task too. They are analytical, to say the least, and you are probably going to get something from them in written form with regards to what is taking place. From work assignments to an invitation, it is going to be thorough so make sure you have your facts straight because they will research you or your company. Though Urchins tend to stay in committed relationships, things have to make sense for them. If things become extremely complicated or unstable, they may be challenged in attempting to stay in a relationship.

Remember, Urchins love information.

Urchins are also strong in the workforce. They are accountants, computer geeks, technicians, company analysts, etc.

Whales

Most people love whales! They want to help everyone almost to a fault, and they are extremely good friends. You can depend on Whales. They will take the time to listen to you. Whales are honest and forthright. One of the down falls of being a Whale is that bad people take advantage of their kindness. To their detriment, Whales sometimes overextend themselves. If Whales could rescue everyone and save the world, they would. You

may have to take a soft approach with whales because of what they have experienced. So many people have abused them and violated their trust that they may take their time establishing relationships.

Whales are observers. They look to see where the problems are and who is in need. Once they see what needs to be done, they will work really hard to take care of it. They are not normally flashy and have very little need to be recognized for what they do for others. Whales have strong long term relationships and tend to be nurturers. Whales sometimes stay in relationships too long because of their level of commitment, but once their trust is broken, it can be hard to rebuild the relationship.

Remember, Whales love to help people.

Profession examples: counselors, pastors, teachers, social workers, missionaries, school teachers, etc.

Sharks

Sharks are the leaders of the bunch. In companies, they are the top producers. And Sharks are in general over achievers and dream chasers. A Shark will eat you alive. If you get in their way, they will run you over to get to what they want. They have no sympathy for you if you are weak and unsure of yourself.

Out of the four personalities, Sharks are probably the most difficult to establish a relationship with but it is possible if you understand how they operate and do not take things personally. A Shark is not going to tip toe around your feelings like a Whale would. They are going to say what they are thinking, when they are thinking it and there is not too much anyone can do to stop them. Sharks are motivated by money, flashy, always flaunts nice things and can be very aggressive. They are ambitious, seek leadership roles and strive to break records. They have no problem talking about themselves and what they have accomplished. They will fight to win. They are not afraid of confrontation or conflict so be prepared if you engage them. You mind as well get straight to the point when talking to a Shark. They do not have time to hear your lullaby. If you are clear about what you want and about what they will get, it will serve them just fine. All they want to know is the bottom-line. Do not sugar coat it, simply tell it like it is. If you present a good opportunity to a Shark, they are all in, and the collaboration will serve you well because of their drive. A Shark would probably respond like Cuba Gooding Jr. in the movie Jerry McGuire, "Show me the money." And if you cannot show a Shark the money, they are probably going to show you the door. Sharks move from one relationship to another easily. They may get bored quickly, or they may not spend as much time as they should with the person they are with because the work,

business, lifestyle, money, and cars are more important than dating.

Remember, a Shark loves to make money.

Profession examples: singers, actors, athletes, doctors, lawyers, salesperson, or incentive driven jobs, etc.

Dolphins

Dolphins are probably the easiest of all of the personalities to get along with. They love to party, and the party loves them. When they walk in, everyone is glad that they showed up. They are fun, smart, witty and full of life. Dolphins are your social butterflies. Being the center of attention is not a problem for them, they love that all eyes are on them. They are just likable people. Dolphins do not put on airs or act stuck up. Dolphins have a knack for including everyone in the fun. Kind of like getting everyone in the pool to play with the ball that is being passed around. Dolphins are usually with their friends and family and spend very little time alone. Dolphins love to attend large venues like VIP parties, concerts, conventions, networking events and black tie affairs.

Remember, Dolphins love to have fun.

Profession examples: radio and television personalities, event promoters, cheerleaders, entrepreneurs, sports commentators, etc.

I hope that you have enjoyed these descriptions. I am sure you either saw yourself or your mate in one or more of the personality types. We all have a dominant personality type, but it is possible that you have a combination of all four types. A personality type is how we act naturally. Your parents saw it in you as a child, and you will see it in your children. You can try to be calm if you are a dolphin but it will not last long. You can try to be loud of you are an Urchin, but that will not last long either. So embrace who you are and learn how to operate with people who possess the other traits.

Let's explain it one more way. This is how the four personality traits say I love you.

- Urchins say "I told you that I loved you when I married you. If I change my mind, I will let you know." They are not being sarcastic. Once they are in, they're in.

- Whales say I love you over and over. It is easy for them. They will say it in public or in private. It is very natural and relaxed for them to express how they feel.

- Sharks rarely say I love you, even if they do you might want them to define what that means. Love declares

commitment; commitment will slow them down, and they cannot have that. Be prepared for that if you are in a relationship with a Shark. The only assurance that you may get is the fact that they have not moved on.

And last but not least, Dolphins. Dolphins are the best when displaying love. After all, they have the most fun right? They will climb on the trunk of a car or stand on a rooftop and yell to the ENTIRE WORLD THAT THEY LOVE YOU!!!! They have no shame. Dolphins will wave a flag with your name on it. Now, to an Urchin that might be overwhelming so just remember that everyone expresses love differently, and you may not get back what you give to them. So if they do not express it the same, it is not that they do not love you, they just express it in their own way. Please do not take it personally.

I hope that by learning how each person operates it will take some of the guessing and emotion out of the relationship process. That you will enjoy what you know about each other and understand each other a little bit more.

Rate Yourself and Your Spouse

YOU

Urchin   _____

Whale   _____

Shark   _____

Dolphin   _____

Total: _____

What percentage would you say that the two of you rank in these personality traits? You should compare notes when you have completed the chart. Do not exceed 100% as your total.

YOUR SPOUSE

Urchin   —————

Whale   —————

Shark   —————

Dolphin   —————

Total: —————

Additional Notes:

_____

_____

_____

_____

Tools Page

What Tools Have You Learned In This Chapter?

_____

_____

_____

_____

_____

_____

_____

_____

_____

_____

_____

_____

_____

_____

_____

_____

_____

_____

_____

_____

_____

8
Who Do You Love

There's something very powerful about allowing another person to live your life with you. To enter your life and walk through the days, months and years together. There's something powerful about two people swimming through time like synchronized swimmers. Winning together, losing together and growing together. I believe that it is extremely important to know how you love personally and how you identify with those you choose to allow to share your space. With that in mind, I'm going to break these areas down in four quadrants to make it simple to understand. This will be similar to the personality types that I explained previously.

Hopefully, this will help you understand why you are attracted to some people and not attracted to others. A

few of the ways that I believe that we can be attracted to someone are physically, mentally, emotionally and intellectually. There may be other attractions like money, prestige, lifestyle or lineage. But those tend to be driven by motive. (Beware of motive driven relationships.) I'd like to focus our attention on the more sincere and loving ways that people encounter and commit to each other.

- Physical attraction can almost be breathtaking. You find this person desirable, and you haven't even met them yet. Their physical features are aesthetically pleasing to you. It could be the way they walk, talk or even smell. We could even call it Aphrodisia, a sexual desire. There is something about them that just does it for you. You cannot explain it, nor do you care to. They are just the type of person that you like. And boy do you like them. If you look back at your past relationships, you can probably find a pattern in the type of person you were attracted to or dated.

- Being mentally attracted to someone means that you are attracted or drawn to them because of their characteristics, mannerisms or habits. They could remind you of one of your parents or siblings. Or there could have been something that you were deprived of in your childhood that is prevalent in their characteristic behavior. That could range from the way they display love, to their communication style. This attraction can

sometimes lead to a codependent relationship because both people can draw off of the other person to balance a deficit. On the other hand, as with the other attractions when dealt with appropriately this can lead to a lasting and loving relationship.

- I am going to say that an emotional attraction is an intense feeling that is generated by your connection to a particular person. That is probably the easiest way that I can break that down. You can say I love you to one person, and you really do care about them, but there is a stronger feeling of emotion when you say it to the person that you have an emotional attraction for. Someone that you like can do something, and it is no big deal, but the same situation has more of an impact on you if you are emotionally attracted to them. And it is hard to determine the onset or reason that we can meet two people who look similar and have similar things to offer, but we become more emotionally attracted to one than the other. The fact is that it happens. And when it does it is a hard connection to break. It can come from the sense of safety, trust, peace, understanding or comfort that you experience with that person. Emotional attraction can yield positive or negative results if not handled properly. All of these attractions can, but it appears that the area of emotion could possibly have a more intense impact if you do not have control over it.

- When you are attracted or drawn to someone intellectually, it means that you are academically and

intellectually inspired when you are with them or when you talk to them. It is stimulating to have a conversation with them. You can bounce things off of each other, and it usually presents and win, win situation for the both of you.

What is very interesting about these four quadrants of attraction are that they can happen at ANY level. You can have two people who are in great shape that are attracted to each other just like you can have to people who struggle to work out that are attracted to each other. And this applies to all four quadrants. Some people may be more intelligent and academically sound or more emotionally in tune than others. And the amazing thing about that is if you tap into this information properly you can enhance your Love System and grow together gracefully.

In most cases, all four quadrants apply to all relationships. Of course, they will weigh out differently for each couple because we are at different points in our lives, at different times. Let's list the attractions and give them a value based on your mate. You are allowed 100 points total for all four attractions. Rank your attraction in each area.

Example:

Physical Attractiveness   _____

Mental Attractiveness   _____

Emotional Attractiveness   _____

Intellectual Attractiveness   _____

                               _____

Total:

Now, these numbers may change over time because we change and grow as people. But usually, though the areas are rarely scored equally you have what you need for the relationship during that period of time. If you find that you are not getting what you need in one of these areas, you need to talk to your mate honestly and lovingly about what you desire. This can help you build

a stronger union and avoid having gaps in areas that can be impacted by other people.

For instance, initially you both had a high school diploma and average jobs. One of you goes back to school and earns a degree which in turn awards you a better job. And the other person is content where they are. Well, now your spouse is having intellectual conversations at work with a woman who understands him and he develops an intellectual and emotional attachment to her. That is why it is important for you to grow together.

I believe that one of the reasons that someone cheats is because someone else is filling one of these four quadrants for them. To assist you in having a successful marriage these quadrants should be addressed, identified with and serviced on a regular basis. If and when we fail to do so, it leaves room for other interest to infiltrate one of the quadrants. For example, spirituality is an emotional and intellectual decision, so it is not exactly a component of the four quadrants, but it can be a derivative for a relationship. You may or may not choose to deal with someone because of their beliefs or how grounded they are in their spiritual walk. What does all of this mean? In an effort to have a fulfilling relationship, it is like a baseball diamond. You want to cover all of the bases. The most effective way to do that is to do a self-check and understand what your needs, wants, and desires are. It is also a good idea to make sure that you

also evaluate how realistic that list is, for you and the expectation that you place on your mate. Once you are sure about that list, the two of you should switch the list and be very clear about the value placed in each quadrant and if you are willing and or able to meet those needs. Compromise is also key in a world where no one gets everything that they want. Be open to truly loving and understanding this person and the process that you will experience together. I am sure that this will pay off.

Tools Page

What Tools Have You Learned In This Chapter?

_____

_____

_____

_____

_____

_____

_____

_____

_____

_____

_____

_____

_____

_____

_____

_____

_____

_____

_____

_____

9
Mastering the Middle Ground

So often we fail to keep our promises to each other. It most often happens with little tiny promises. You want to be a Promise Keeper. Promises that you didn't even realize that you made can cause damage. Words that sounded like general conversation to you but translated into promises to your mate can change everything. I know that you are probably saying that you always keep your promises, but I would beg to differ. There is a thing called unintentional promises. An unintentional promise is something that is spoken when the two of you are having a general conversation, while the two of you are joking or when you are telling a story to each other or to someone else.

Let me give you an example. You and your wife are walking in the grocery store, and you pass another couple accompanied by the husband's mother. The mother is giving the wife a very hard time. You can see the pain on the wife's face as the husband kind of shrugs like "you know how my mom is." The two of you look at each other and not knowing what else to say your husband says to you; " I would never let my mother treat you like that." The wife gently places her arm in his arm sweetly and securely locked at the elbow, and they continue shopping and laughing as normal. This is what the husband does not understand; she takes comfort in knowing that her husband would never allow that to happen to her. For her, this has established a level of trust in him and in their relationship. She feels safe, secure and nothing will come between them. And if by chance it does, he is going to handle that like *Johnny on the spot* because that is the kind of man he is. That is the kind of man that she is married to. She is so proud, and she will tell her girlfriends, and anyone else that will listen that she has a good man and no one, not even his mother will come before her.

A year and a half later the two of them have a son. Her mother-in-law comes to stay with them and what happens? Her husband sees a side of his mother that he has never seen before. A nagging, irritable, know it all grandmother. He looks at his wife's pain stricken face with the same look that the other husband had in the

grocery store before. And in response, he gives her the same face and shrug that say, "You know how my mom is." The wife is in utter disbelief, and she feels betrayed. How could he do this to me? I thought I was more important to him than that. And last but not least she thinks; he promised me this would never happen.

Well, he didn't let it happen. He had no idea that one day he would be the man he saw in the store. He never anticipated that this would ever come back to haunt him, and now that it has, it looks like he did not keep his word, if he even remembers that he said it at all. He has no idea what to do. He is probably thinking, what in the world is going on with my mother. And the big mistake he is about to make, and most men make, is assuming that your wife will be more understanding than his mother. Wrong! She is not more understanding; she is quiet because she is trying to figure out what in the world is happening to her. And now this couple is on the slow road to miscommunication if one of them does not pull the reigns.

Haven't you had something like that happen to you? If you are dating maybe you said I love you too soon, or maybe you started out early saying that you wanted to get married. You were at a family dinner, and someone announced their engagement and in your excitement and haste you said, "That is great. We are getting engaged soon too." Her sister overheard you and runs and pulls your girlfriend in the bathroom and says, "He is about to

propose. I just heard it with my own ears." Your lady is so happy, and she knows that February, the month to propose; is right around the corner. Things are going great between the two of you. As time passes, you realized you might need to wait a little while longer to clear up some things before you get married. You had never mentioned getting married to her. That was a general conversation that you had in passing at a family dinner. You have no idea she has been waiting for you to keep your word. You have to because you said it in front of her family. Well, in essence; you lied. Not intentionally, because at the time that might have been exactly how you felt. But now she still feels the same, and you feel differently because you have some things that you want to be resolved first. She has told her entire family and all of her friends that she has finally met Mr. Right Now, and you realized that you might have rushed in too quickly. I may be exaggerating a bit, but I wanted to give you an example of how people make unintentional promises.

Let's talk about some of the things that may have been said after you were engaged or married. You are married, and she may have said in conversation that this was your last child, and you depended on that because you wanted her all to yourself even though you love your children. You begin to mentally plan out your vacations and how you are going to turn the basement into your man cave. And then, after your youngest child's 15th

birthday party, she stares out of the window in the kitchen watching him talk to his friends. You see a look you haven't seen before, and you ask her what is wrong. And she says "I cannot believe how fast he grew up." With a big grin on your face, you say "Time is flying." And the only thing you are thinking about is that big screen TV you are going to place on the wall in your man cave. She looks at you and doesn't even see the happiness oozing out of you and says, "All of the other kids are out of the house, and soon he will be gone too. Honey, I really want another child." You have no clue what to say. Between the look on her face and your personal desires, you feel a little betrayed. We have raised our family. I did everything that you wanted me to do as a husband and father. I just wanted some time for us, and you want to start all over again. She just broke an unintentional promise that she spoke casually one night at a dinner with friends that he had logged away and counted on.

And let us not forget intimacy. A woman describes to her man what sex will look like during their marriage. Of course, that is something that people should discuss. Maybe she says something like; I am extremely sexually active, and once we get married, we will have a great sex life. Or she may say that she is not the type to withhold sex if you two have a disagreement. Well, he counts on that, and he is not happy when he finds out after they are married, that her definition of an extremely active sex

life and his definition of an extremely active sex life are two different definitions.

What about when a man tells his wife that his goal is to make sure that she does not have to work after a few years, and she ends up retiring from her job at age 65 because he always wanted to buy a bigger house or a new boat. Well, that would mean that, that never happened.

I know that some of these stories made you laugh or may have even sounded very familiar to you, but these are some of the things that happen in relationships. You are probably asking yourself how can these simple to discuss but yet controversial topics and issues be handled or avoided. I have such an easy answer for you. You are not going to believe what I use to help couples avoid making unintentional promises to each other. Are you ready? Here goes.

The rule is: *It is your responsibility to discuss with your mate anything directly or indirectly spoken that is important to you.*

If your mate says something, and it is something that means a lot to you or it is something that establishes an agreement or understanding on how you are going to operate as a couple or be treated, you need to have a very clear conversation with them.

The conversation should include the following:

1. You want to share what you heard.
2. They should, in turn, share what they said.
3. You want to share what that meant to you.
4. They should, in turn, share what it meant to them.
5. What is our joint understanding or expectation on this topic?

It is important that after you both have a clear understanding of where you stand on the topic that you also clarify any expectations that either of you has. If you both know what the expectations are, then you are both now aware of the impact it has on your relationship. The great thing about this is that you can add this to your love system. It will not be uncommon or uncomfortable for you to talk about these issues and find a middle ground. It may even cause you to have a better understanding when future conversations arise because you will learn more about how the other person thinks and what their needs are.

You are going to hear several different reasons why couples end up divorced. Much of it stems back to the couple not really getting to know each other or not having clear and realistic expectations of each other

before getting married. A couple may also initially do a great job of getting to know each other but as they grow they fail to implement the same strategy they used, in the beginning, to adequately support the relationship as it advances. When these strategies are not utilized, and the vastly different needs are not met, challenges may arise. To avoid the compounding effect that negative thoughts and feelings can have in a relationship, it is a great idea to keep the lines of communication open and reiterate the needs and expectations of both people.

Tools Page

What Tools Have You Learned In This Chapter?

_____

_____

_____

_____

_____

_____

_____

_____

_____

_____

_____

_____

_____

_____

_____

_____

_____

_____

10
Relationship Building Blocks

Philosophy is what governs the direction of a relationship. It is key to decide and discuss what your philosophy is going to be for your union. Philosophy is when you develop a set of ideas or a standard for how you are going to live your life, raise your family and accomplish your goals. You may say that you have not developed a philosophy as of yet. Well, I am going to say that you have. You just did not know that is what you were doing. If you look at how you are living your life right now, you will see that how you operate or the lack there of is a result of your personal philosophy. Good, bad or indifferent. The great thing about your philosophy is that you can always change and improve it and therefore impact the results it yields. So if this is the first time that you have thought about this,

it is okay. You just start from where you are and design a new philosophy that suits where you would like to end up.

With that being said, now that you know where you both stand individually as far as your philosophy is concerned you want to develop a joint or family philosophy. The philosophy that the two of you develop together will mold your children, drive or drain your finances and build or destroy your marriage. It is just that simple. How flexible you are with each other, how eager you both are to find a common place of understanding or how much pride either of you operate in while developing this family philosophy can make all of the difference in the world as to how this marriage and your family turns out. So it is vitally important for you to take this very seriously. Give it some sincere thought and yield to the mission at hand, not your ego.

When developing this philosophy, keep in mind that you want it to work for both of you and that it does not matter who is right or wrong. This philosophy will give you some structure and direction. It will guide you in your most challenging battles and protect you when opposition rises against your family. Your philosophy will make you proud of your marriage and overtime it may need to be adjusted as your journey together continues.

Together this idea or standard will take you as far as you have the courage to travel and I hope that is a beautiful endless road.

Boundaries

There are certain boundaries that you should discuss and implement before you get married. A few examples are:

1. The types of relationships that you have with other people. Especially if there was a prior relationship with them.
2. The way we communicate with other people; an example is using pet names or displaying forms of affection. I am a hugger, so I keep in mind that everyone is not like me. And I always consider appropriateness like the setting or venue, personal, professional and relational impact.
3. The time we spend with other people.
4. The type of money decisions we will make alone and together.
5. Who you allow to be involved in your relationship or whose opinion we heed to.
6. Respecting each other's privacy and what you discuss with others.
7. Protecting each other's reputation.
8. Mind trap of conversations. As referenced when we talked about communication.

Be sure to carefully set and clarify your boundaries. Be patient with each other as you redesign your external relationships. One of you may move quickly, and the other may wait for situations to arise that extend an opportunity to communicate the changes. Either way, work together and do allow anything external to impact what you are building internally.

Handling Conflict

Conflict can be so damaging that you have to remember to handle each other with care. So many couples experience divorce over what I would like to call unfinished conversations. You might be asking yourself what that means. An unfinished conversation is an argument. I call that an unfinished conversation because tensions are high, rational thought, and reasoning are both absent and in most instances, both people think that they are either right or have been wronged because if that were not the truth, there wouldn't have been an argument in the first place.

When you argue, no one can hear the other person's true point of view. You are having a conversation that will not be resolved. People say things that they do not

mean or would not normally say. They hurt each other with their words and make statements that they can never retrieve. When nothing is or can be resolved the opportunity to communicate is deserted. Nothing comes out of it but ammunition for the next fight. Neither person will forget the words that were spoken and fueled by anger. And to add insult to injury, the couple will not resolve what started the argument in the first place. And now we have unfinished business.

I am going to ask you to try something. Just hear me out. The next time you get upset about something I want you to take a piece of paper and write down what you are upset about. Not in all capital letters like you are yelling. No exclamation marks like you are screaming. Just simply write down what you are upset about. Read it once every hour for the next 3 hours. If you are still upset after 3 hours, then give the note to your spouse. They have the same amount of time to flip over the note and write a response to your issue. No one is allowed to use this as an opportunity to bring up their issue about something else in the response. You can only address the issue at hand. Once they respond you both decide when you are going to talk about it keeping in mind that you do not leave for work or go to bed angry. And you should both be prepared to have a resolve and if necessary an explanation.

This tactic defuses anger and makes you think about what you are saying to the person that you love because

you have to write it down. And guess what that means? You have finished the conversation. No unfinished business here.

Now, I must add that even if this works you have to remember to stay committed to the resolution. Couples end up fighting over repeat issues because the same situations arise over and over. You cannot just simply apologize and do the same thing again. That expresses that you did not really mean it when you apologized. ***The greatest apology to the person you say you love is a change in behavior.*** There is nothing like a man or woman feeling valued because you sincerely took their feelings into consideration and truly changed your behavior in that area. That shows them how important they are, and it will add miles to your wonderful union. You can put some steps in place to ensure this is successful like; Properly Identifying the Issue, Commit to a Resolve and Establish a Follow Up Process.

Fighting Fair or Not at All

At some point, everyone might encounter some heated fellowship, or in layman's terms, fight. It is important to understand what you are fighting for. Remember you are not fighting each other. You are learning how to communicate in the midst of disagreement or transition in an effort to avoid causing damage to your marriage.

Most people believe that the war is in the divorce. You are fighting over the children, what you have built together and what you own separately. But do you know that the real fight is in the marriage, not the divorce? That's right. The fight begins long before you are fed up with each other. You should collectively in action and deed, be fighting for a loving, fruitful and productive marriage.

You should be fighting for the lives of your children and the sanctity of your home. And you should be fighting for the heart and health of your mate. Outside issues threaten the core of the love that the two of you confess to each other, so let's wage a counter attack by finding ways to communicate issues with grace. Here is a tool that might help you with that.

Are You Being FAIR?

Often times when we are in a relationship and we attempt to discuss a topic or resolve an issue; emotions run high, and we find ourselves in a crisis. One of the ways that we can come up with an amicable resolution or have a positive outcome is to be FAIR. I am sure your mind just thought about 100 ways that your spouse or fiancé has not been FAIR but before you shift the blame or start making your list let's look at what FAIR really is.

- **F – Faith**: Are your decisions inspired by the word of God? Is your faith guiding how you handle your spouse or fiancé? Resolving situations and having conversations with God as the head of your life along with his guidance will equip you to respond properly to your spouse or fiancé. It will also allow you to listen to their point of view even if what they have to say is hard to hear. Wanting God's best for them will cause you to evaluate your response in an effort not to have a negative outcome. We should all believe in something. Have faith.

- **A – Admiration**: Are you handling the conversation or issue in a way that makes your spouse or fiancé feel loved, esteemed, appreciated or admired? If your spouse or fiancé is feeling beat down or unappreciated it may be a little difficult to get and keep their attention or have them buy into what you are attempting to discuss. Choose your words carefully. Words have wings, and you cannot get them back once spoken.

- **I – Integrity**: Are you being honest? Be upfront with your spouse or fiancé about what is really going on. The worst thing you can do is to have them make a decision based on inaccurate or incorrect information. In the long run, neither of you will get what you want, and trust is one of the hardest things to repair. If they love

you, the hope is that they will work through it with you and if they are not in love with you, you need to know that for your own good. For goodness sake, if you're hurt say that you're hurt and why. If there is a financial issue, say there is a financial issue. If you make a mistake say you made a mistake. If they are really for you it will all work out; I once heard it said that "You cannot say the wrong thing to the right person!" If they are the right person, then they are already on the ship called "LOVE" with you in calm or turbulent waters. On the other hand, if you are the recipient of such information be careful not to betray their trust when responding to their honesty. If you fail in your response, it may be hard to get them to confide in you again. And please delete from your vocabulary the old statement of "I told you so." It may be the last time you are able to respond to them that way because it may cause them to shut down completely. Ask each other the question? "Can I trust you with what has happened in my life and with how I feel, now and in the future? Can I trust you with my truth?" Think about it carefully before you answer because if you say yes, when they come to you your "YES" still has to be and respond like a "YES."

• **R – Respect:** Does your spouse or fiancé feel respected when you make decisions or deal with other people. One of the pitfalls of relationships is the deficit of respect. Disrespect devalues your spouse or fiancé and

sometimes can cause huge gaps in your communication. Think about how what you're about to do or say will impact or affect the one you love.

So now I ask you again; are you being **FAIR?**

Overlooked Triggers of Conflict

Tolerance

Tolerance can be misleading because it gives the appearance that there is not an issue or on the other hand, that the issue is bigger than what it actually is. Everyone has a different tolerance level, and that is what can make things tricky.

I was involved in a car accident to no fault of my own, and my neck and back were injured. Unfortunately, I had been involved in car accidents before and experienced an extreme amount of pain. This time, it did not feel as bad. I thought that the treatment would not take as long this time and that I would heal faster than before. This injury was nowhere as near as bad as the last one. About three weeks into my treatment I was experiencing some prolonging discomfort. I told my physical therapist, and he decided to do a heat and massage treatment on my neck and upper back. As he began to press, he stopped and said, "Dawn, how much pain are you in?" And I said its constant but I can stand it. He began to massage more and press and in doing so

I almost wanted to cry. The pressure that he was applying was exposing the magnitude of the injury. Now, I knew the pain was there, but it was not until the pressure was applied that I now realize how injured I really was.

My physical therapist began to give me instructions and an explanation. What hit me more than anything was his shock that I was not affected by it like most people he treated normally are. And this is what he said to me. "Dawn, the knots are compounded. How are you standing and not buckling in pain? I am going to have to use the machine for you because they are so bad that you will mess up my hands and end my PT career. It is just that bad. If there was an award for the worst case I have seen, today you would win it." After he was done and left the room, I cried as I was getting dressed. Of course, I could not let him see me cry from the pain. Pride. But I could hear him sharing with the staff how bad my back was. When I came out to grab my schedule for the next appointment the administrator looked at me with such empathy based on his verbal expression of concern for me. She said "Dawn, you have to follow all the instructions and get better. No one should be walking around like that." This is important because it speaks to my tolerance for pain. Physically and emotionally my tolerance I would say is about the same. I have always been able to operate injured because I have been through

physical and emotional trials all of my life. So I have a very high tolerance for pain.

Now that can be positive and negative. Remember the personality types that we talked about previously in the book? Well, I am a combination of all four. I am a Whale (I love people), with a Dolphin nature (I would be the one on your job with coffee and music at 5 in the morning, getting on your nerves), an Urchins inquisitiveness (I want the facts and the information) and a Sharks drive (Show me the money. Let's go to work.)

You can have a little or a lot of all four types. With that being said, like a Whale I have a higher tolerance for people while they are in their process, probably more than some other people do or would have. But like injured Whales, once I am done, I am done. I have also dealt with health challenges since I was a child and that also has garnered my high tolerance for physical pain. I am saying that to say that good or bad; I tolerate more than a lot of my peers. Call it empathy or understanding; I am guilty.

Now, how does that fair for me in relationships? That would depend on the motive of the other party. If they are a good person who sincerely cares about me, it turns out great. But if it is someone that has a negative motive, then there is a chance that someone is going to get hurt or taken advantage of. The same applies to you and your mate. You might confuse their high level of tolerance with the level of positive or negative impact that you are

having in their life. You over spend, speak roug
fail to keep your word about something and they
to respond or very tolerant towards you. You m
mistake of thinking that either what you are doing _ not
so bad or that it does not bother them. You might even
think that they are a push over. Nevertheless, you keep
on operating in the same behavior and even though they
speak to you kindly about the issues you just take for
granted that it is okay. Then one day your understanding
mate says they need space, or they want out. Now you
do not understand what's going on with your push over.
Well, their tolerance was high for your foolishness but
everything eventually fills the cup, and they are done
trying to tell you how they should be treated. By the time
you get to counseling, they are not even the person you
remember. They are withdrawn and not even slightly
impacted by your apology.

Now the opposite holds true for someone with low
tolerance. They tell you how they feel once or twice and
the next time you do something that they feel is out of
order, they are out of there. I am sure there are some
people who are in between those two extremes. If you're
getting to know your mate try to evaluate how they
process their emotions and what their tolerance level is.
Both of you should evaluate what you tolerate and why
you tolerate it. Or why you have a very low tolerance for
some things and a high tolerance for other things.

Sometimes couples have challenges because one person may feel like they are being taken advantage of. It is up to both of you to discover your mate's tolerance level and discuss your own. It would be a good idea to add how you are going to deal with each other's tolerance to your Love System.

Betrayal

Some people would say that betrayal is more prominent with women than it is for men. I do not necessarily agree with that. I think that the displeasure of the betrayal may be expressed more with women than it is with men because to a man, expressing it might show his vulnerability, and he cannot have that. So I believe the impact and the outcome of the betrayal may be the same; it is simply displayed differently.

Betrayal is the breaking or violation of a presumptive contract, trust, or confidence that produces moral and psychological conflict within a relationship amongst individuals, between organizations or between individuals and organizations. Examples like giving information about (a person, group, country, etc.) to an enemy. To hurt (someone who trusts you, such as a friend or relative) by not giving help or by doing something morally wrong. To show (something, such as

a feeling or desire) without wanting or trying to. To lead astray; especially seduce.

Betrayal is from the root word betray, which comes from the Middle English word bitrayen — meaning "mislead, deceive." Betrayal has to do with destroying someone's trust, possibly by lying. If you start dating your best friend's girlfriend behind his back, that's an act of betrayal. Betrayal can also mean "helping an enemy," such as a person who gives secret information to a country that is at war with his or her own country.

It is very hard to resolve betrayal. Once a couple arrives here it takes a lot for me to get them back on the same page. Try to avoid this obstacle by any means possible. How do you do that? By having a clear understand of what loyalty and commitment mean to both of you. Remember that it is about the level of importance to each individual. Make your perspective known to each other; if not someone may feel minimized. Once you have betrayed someone the fastest but most uncomfortable way back is honesty, because you have to expose your lies. You can ruin any hopes of restoration if you continue to be dishonest.

Tension

Tension is defined as mental and emotional strain or to apply force to something that tends to stretch it. We see the tension in so many areas of our lives. We see racial

tension, financial tension, political tension and emotional tension. We are constantly pulled in various directions based on the force that is negatively applied to our lives by tension.

We take sides in varies situations based on tension (mental and emotional strain). We find ourselves exhausted because of tension (the force that is applied in order to stretch something). Tension has caused us to end relationships, leave jobs and dissolve marriages. Tension has divided countries, created wars and destroyed companies. So what can we learn from a force that is ever present and extremely effective in its pursuit to destroy love, peace, abundance, unity and mankind?

I believe that tension starts internally before it becomes evident externally. If we are settled ourselves, then it is harder for others to frustrate us. Take the time to reflect on the philosophy that you designed as a couple. Settle yourself on those beliefs and stay focused on what you will benefit by being committed to those beliefs and your relationship. Relieve the tension in your life by pursuing and relying on your personal faith. That will center you and bring you comfort. Deal with your internal fires and issues. When you work on your root issues and honestly deal with your personal challenges the transformation in your relationships, finances and situations will be evidence that you have grown in those areas. It will help to relieve the tension and allow you to move forward with each other.

Unforgiveness

If we are in a relationship that has experienced some challenges, then we know that in order to move forward we must forgive. When we stay in a relationship, and we have not forgiven the person, everything becomes a trigger. On the other hand, if you know that you do not want a relationship or even a friendship with someone you still need to forgive them. But do not confuse forgiveness with reestablishing the relationship. Forgiveness is an act of the heart.

Once you release it, you do not have to prove to anyone that you have done so. Sometimes people want you to prove that you have forgiven them by reestablishing the relationship. Forgiveness does not mean reconciliation. It means that you hold no issue with them and release their effect on you. When you forgive someone, that does not negate consequences. They still very well might lose a good friend and what could have potentially been a good relationship. Do not be pressured into granting someone access to you who has proven that they are not responsible enough or mature enough for the relationship. Forgive them and move on if necessary because forgiveness is for you. If you are married, when you forgive each other, start off with a clean slate; leaving the issues, the pain and the past behind you.

Tools Page

What Tools Have You Learned In This Chapter?

_____

_____

_____

_____

_____

_____

_____

_____

_____

_____

_____

_____

_____

_____

_____

_____

_____

_____

_____

_____

11
The Numbers

When you look at the statistics with regards to divorce it can make you a little uneasy about the possibility of having a successful marriage that you can enjoy. I include these statistics not to discourage you but to encourage you not to become one of these numbers. For every person who divorces there is a person who did not divorce their spouse. In 2010 the divorce rate was 36% then that means 64% of the marriages made it. I want you to end up in the 64%.

The impact of divorce may cause both individuals to experience financial hardships and a change in living conditions. If the issue that you allowed to cause you to get a divorce is not worth losing your current lifestyle, changing your living arraignments and possibly losing

some regular access to your children why are we allowing the issue to win? We have to do a better job of fighting the right fight. The fight is against the challenge or issue; the fight is not against your mate. The fight is against the outside influences that threaten your happiness and the stability of your family. Not against your husband or wife. If you could take the emotion, disappointment or frustration out of the situation long enough to see who the real enemy is, what the real problem is and attack the problem instead of your other half it would literally change the game.

It is time for you to weigh the value of the relationship against the weight of losing your future. So many times I have helped couples see that the effort they are putting into fighting with each other is far more than the issue deserves. But when we are hurt, and pain is motivating or intensifying our actions we often fail to handle things appropriately.

It is time for you to choose what is more important. Being right, making the other person suffer like they make you suffer or feel the way you feel or taking the high road and working through the problem so that you can have the life you married them to have. You married them for a reason. Is the problem you are having now worth that reason? I am guessing that it isn't. I am guessing that you just want things to work out but you feel helpless. I am guessing that you really want it to go back to the way it was, but you are embarrassed because

someone already may know what has taken place. Well, I encourage you to hold on. People will be on to something else in no time. Someone else will be the topic of conversation soon, and everything will be fine.

I hope that one of you will have the courage to ask the other not to give up on your marriage. That one of you will stop divorce dead in its tracks, take pride off of the table and with all of your heart apologize and ask for another chance. I want to hear your success story, and I want you to be able to say I am one of the marriages that made it. I am one of the 64%.

Divorce Statistics in America for Marriage

Marriage	Divorce statistics (in percent)
First Marriage	45% to 50% marriages end in divorce
Second Marriage	60% to 67% marriages end in divorce
Third Marriage	70% to 73% marriages end in divorce

* Source of this Divorce Statistics: Jennifer Baker, Forest Institute of Professional Psychology, Springfield

Enrichment Journal also gives similar divorce statistics in America:

- The divorce rate in America for first marriage is 41%
- The divorce rate in America for second marriage is 60%
- The divorce rate in America for third marriage is 73%

Marriage Unbreakable
The War Against Divorce

Children of Divorce Statistics

According to discovery channel, couples with children have a slightly lower rate of divorce than childless couples. Sociologists also believe that childlessness is also a common cause of divorce. The absence of children leads to loneliness and weariness. In the United States, at least 66 per cent of all divorced couples are childless.

Divorcing Couples	Divorce Rate Statistics (in percent)
Couples With Children	40%
Couples Without Children	66%

* Source of this Divorce Statistics: Discover Channel

Per capita divorce rate statistics from 1990 to 2010

Year	Per Capita Divorce Rate Statistics
1991	0.47%
1992	0.48%
1993	0.46%
1994	0.46%
1995	0.46%
1996	0.43%
1997	0.43%
1998	0.42%
1999	0.41%

2000	0.41%
2001	0.40%
2002	0.39%
2003	0.38%
2004	0.37%
2005	0.36%
2006	0.37%
2007	0.36%
2008	0.35%
2009	0.35%
2010	0.36%

* Source of this Divorce Statistics: Americans for Divorce Reform

Provisional number of divorces and annulments and rate: United States, 2000-2010

Year	Divorces and Annulments	Population	Rate per 1,000 total population
2010	872000	244122529	3.6
2009	840000	242610561	3.5
2008	844000	240545163	3.5
2007	856000	238352850	3.6
2006	872000	236094277	3.7

2005	847000	233495163	3.6
2004	879000	236402656	3.7
2003	927000	243902090	3.8
2002	955000	243108303	3.9
2001	940000	236416762	4
2000	944000	233550143	4

• Excludes data for California, Georgia, Hawaii, Indiana, Louisiana, and Minnesota

Tools Page

What Tools Have You Learned In This Chapter?

_____

_____

_____

_____

_____

_____

_____

_____

_____

_____

_____

_____

_____

_____

_____

_____

_____

_____

_____

12
Stay Close to Each Other

We have saved the best for last. Or at least some of you will think so. We have talked about everything from family to communication, and now we are going to talk about intimacy. In a world full of busyness it is very important that you two stay close to each other and develop and bond of deep intimacy. Intimacy is a state marked by 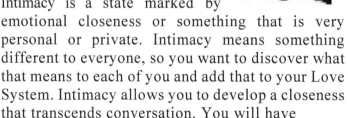 emotional closeness or something that is very personal or private. Intimacy means something different to everyone, so you want to discover what that means to each of you and add that to your Love System. Intimacy allows you to develop a closeness that transcends conversation. You will have

unspoken signals that simply develop out of your loving bond. Intimacy allows you to have conversations that you could never have before. Intimacy will open up doors to your marriage that no one else can walk through.

As you begin to discover this special closeness, new opportunities to love each other will arise. And it can be from the way you two lean on each other to the passion in your love making. You may call it intimacy in different terms like holding and touching each other while he calls it relief. You could rely on intimacy because it makes you feel comforted, loved and secure while simultaneously he could rely on intimacy because it relieves his stress and takes the weight off his day or his problems. It means something different to each person but if you know what it means then you can make sure that desire is met for each of you.

The many ways that people describe intimacy are loving verbal communication, making love, holding hands, provision, eye contact, encouragement, and even personal massages. There are no real answers for this. You know what makes you feel connected and close to someone. I've even heard someone say that sharing their faith and prayer was very intimate and impactful for them. It just depends on the person, but whatever it is, you should know. And you should be the only one that experiences this special place with your spouse.

Let's talk about it....... Sex

I am a Christian, and we can experience ridicule when we talk about certain things, but I am going on in anyway. In other words, I'm going to talk about sex. I believe that if you do not talk about sex and intimacy with your spouse, someone else will. Therefore, you need to have an intinate and indept conversation about sex in your marriage. I say this because we know that affairs are at the top of the list when we talk about the issues that challenge your union. I am going to get straight to the point, and I hope that the fact that I am going to be very candid will help someone. It will at least save me some time since I am not going to tap dance around it.

We have talked about the four types of attractions,  and we have talked about the needs of your mate. Now we need to talk about what I am going to call the sexual appetite. This is a private matter and should only be discussed between you and your spouse, but it NEEDS to be discussed. There is a difference between having an attraction for your spouse and having a sexual appetite. I cannot tell you how many people do not understand why their spouse is cheating because intimately they are great together. When

unless they are just a cheater by nature, and yes women cheat too; it is probably that their sexual appetite is greater than yours, and someone else has tapped into that need. You may be okay with twice a week, and they may need it every day. I always joke with the women that I counsel, and I tell them from the gate. You better find out what his appetite is, especially since some of us have been saving ourself for marriage. And if she has been waiting five years and he only wants to make love once a week, she is going to find herself praying a lot. And if he would like to make love every day and she thinks that is too much, they are going to have some issues. I know that I make this sound humorous, but it is really serious.

If you have two people who love each other, and they are both attracted to each other, they will probably have a great sex life, but if one of them is yearning for more intimacy and someone else taps into that need, there is going to be a problem. You have probably heard that sex is different for men than it is for women. That may be true, but your sex drive is your sex drive whether you are a woman or a man. Because our bodies are designed to respond to touch and stimulation someone who really does not want to cheat may find themselves trapped between their sex drive and their faithfulness. The number one way to

avoid that is to make sure your mate's needs are met but there are also some other things that you need to understand to avoid falling into the cheating trap. First, having self-discipline and boundaries are obviously great ways to stay on track in your marriage so everyone should strive to handle themselves with that in mind, to avoid these traps all together.

Three of the things that I have discovered over the years while counseling couples that have led them down the wrong road as it pertains to faithfulness are:

- Communication
- Interaction
- Opportunity

Once these three things happen it is almost probable that someone if going to cheat. Remember that earlier in the book we talked about communication. We talked about how it formed alliances and that you should commit to having the strongest communication with your spouse. Well, this is one of the reasons why. Communication forms alliances and you should not have any alliances with anyone that could compromise your marriage. Therefore, cut that chit chatting out, just to add a little humor to such a touchy subject. Small conversations lead to longer and more intimate conversations. Save yourself early and end those conversations before they go too far. Once you start

having those conversations, they will inevitably lead to interaction, a face to face. I can tell you so many one liners that lead to this, but I do not have the time to discuss them. But I will say that once a conversation hits this point, the other person probably knows its coming and they are ready to say yes. And here we go, once there is conversation and interaction; opportunity is lying in wait. Waiting for the first time that no one is around so it can take advantage of the foundation that communication and interaction have laid. Sometimes this happens over time. Sometimes this happens quickly. I cannot pinpoint the exact time frame but what I do know, is that it happens. And unfortunately, it happens often. More often than any of us would hope. That is why you have to be very careful about having someone of the opposite sex as your confidant. I am not saying that it is impossible to do, I am just saying you have to be very careful who you have that kind of communication and trust with outside of your marriage.

We are all going to be attracted to someone even after we are married. It is not the attraction that is the issue; it is our lack of maturity in responding to the attraction that causes problems. We have these wonderful body parts called eyes that allow us to see what we desire and those amazing ears that allow us to hear loving words. So we have to be very careful how we respond to what we see and what we hear. When we are aware of these pitfalls, and we have the appropriate

boundaries in place, we safe guard our marriage, protect our spouse and our family.

So how can you open up the dialogue on such a sensitive topic? Especially if you are already married and might personally think that you have a great sex life. Just ask each other if you are fulfilled intimately. Maybe making love is great but one of you would like it more often, or there is a way that you enjoy it more. There may even be something that you have not discovered together yet. Just be honest. And if by chance you find that there is something that one of you may not enjoy, share that too.

For instance, most men are like tea kettles and most women are like crock pots. Tea kettles only take a few minutes to boil up but crock pots take hours before the meal is ready. So if a man comes home and is ready to make love and his wife is pushing him off saying "Baby, I have to cook" or any other excuse it's because you have not called her all day. She has not received any affection from you and now you want to go straight to bed. She is a crock pot. Call her, text her, surprise her; do something. Those little things will take you a long way men. But if you haven't loved on her all day and then you just jump right to it you may not get the satisfaction that you want. Have you ever had that happen, and then after you hugged at dinner and helped her in the kitchen or with the kids, she was raring to go? You loved on her, and now she cannot wait to love on you. So if you know that

all day at work, the only thing you are thinking about is getting home to her, then start sending her notes or give her a loving call and watch how much easier it is to connect intimately with each other when you get home.

Remember that women are receivers. You will get back from them, whatever you give them for the most part; with all of us keeping mind that we are all still growing ourselves. If you give them love, you will get a warm, loving and receptive home in return. If you show them that they can trust you, you will have more freedom without any concern because they are secure when you two are apart. If you give them resources, they will find ways to better your lives. But if you cheat on them, you will not have a peaceful environment in your home because they will give you back sadness, anger, and disappointment. If you speak down to them and do not spend time with them, it will cause them to shut down emotionally and intimately because they will feel neglected or abused.

Men have so much power in a relationship. The way a man carries himself governs the direction and course of his relationships, family and success. A man invokes, creates or determines change, good or bad. If you honor yourself, your marriage and your money, those things have no choice but to return positive results to you. Likewise, if you dishonor those things, they will return negative results to you. Let me say it like this; you cannot break the laws of the universe that God has placed us in

and expect to receive positive results. For instance, the laws of love, integrity, and honor. In other words, you cannot expect the laws that you break to serve you. If you do not honor them, you will receive no honor from them. This is why you are wondering what is going on with the plans you had for greatness, as you look at the sum total of your life. Check to see if you are breaking the laws that you expect to produce for you. As the head, you resolve problems, you call out the conflict between you and your wife, and you ensure that everything in your realm of responsibility is safe and provided for. And your help will come from that which you honor. Your wife, your family, your friends and your financial resources. This philosophy applies to all of us, so we should all take heed but the man is the first human God physically placed on the earth, and everything in the earth was designed to support him. If we could get back to that premise, we would truly be pleased with our lives. In the meantime, we can all male and female alike do all we can, to be the best we can, so we have the life we plan. Everyone needs to play their role, take ownership and be accountable for their decisions while developing their character.

These are not all of the answers. You will get to know your spouse so you will come up with ideas together but I hope these tips help. Just make an attempt to love each other more than you do anything else. If you both focus on each other's need, then it will not leave

room for someone else to. Remember, marriage is an airplane, and once it takes flight, none is getting off so let's make it a smooth flight.

In Closing ....
If All Else Fails

No one gets married to get divorced. Riding off into to the sunset and building the house with a white picket fence is more in line with what most people hope for concerning marriage. We want it to last. But if you find yourself dissolving your marriage, or you have picked up this book, and you are already divorced, take heart. Just like anything else, you can begin again. I hope that no one ends up here, but if you do, be encouraged that what you have learned in the past will help you have a more successful relationship in the future. I would like to suggest that you consider your children and your family when you deal with each other. That you attempt to co-parent with integrity and provide a verbally safe environment for your childrens as it pertains to how you converse about the other parent. This can be a long road depending on the ages of your children, but you can do it. You can be model parents, and you can get married again. Read the chapters in the book that talk about being single and adjust your perspective. You can live and love again.

Epilogue

In the beginning of this book we talked about all of the books that are out there that you can use for tools to build a better marriage. I hope that what you have read within these pages added to those tools and has intrigued you about your spouse. At the end of the day, the most important thing that you can do is talk to each other. Be open, be honest and be intimate in every sense of the word. Take the time to make the investment in your mate and fight for your marriage. You two are one, and every aspect of your life should look like it.

You have more access to your spouse than anyone else. You are the one who encourages them or the one who discourages them. Your words give them life or tear them down. He needs your respect, and she needs your love. You can make them feel safe, or your actions take their security away. The great thing is that you have control of your relationship, and you can guide the ship wherever you want.

I know that you can avoid divorce and live a life you love. Will you take the challenge and become one of the Strongest Marriages in America?

Tools Page

What Tools Have You Learned In This Chapter?

_____

_____

_____

_____

_____

_____

_____

_____

_____

_____

_____

_____

_____

_____

_____

_____

_____

_____

_____

Tools Page

What Tools Have You Learned In This Chapter?

_____

_____

_____

_____

_____

_____

_____

_____

_____

_____

_____

_____

_____

_____

_____

_____

_____

_____

_____

_____

Reader's Study Guide

Lesson One: The Greatest Gift

1 Everyone has different views of what a healthy relationship looks like. Based on what you have experienced in your family or what you have been exposed to, how do you view your ideal mate?

_____

_____

_____

2 What would you like to incorporate into your marriage that is a part of your culture or something that you have enjoyed or appreciated in your family?

_____

_____

_____

_____

3 Do you understand the value that marriage brings to your life? What you contribute to someone else's life and what they contribute to yours?

_____

_____

_____

_____

Lesson Two: A Love System

1   When you tell your husband or wife (present or to be) that you love them, are you committed to never changing your emotional position concerning them regardless of their failures and human flaws?

_____

_____

_____

_____

2   Real love grants permission to the other party to affect or impact your life and the lives of those you love and that love you. Discuss what this means to both of you.

_____

_____

_____

_____

3   A Love System is a system defined as any formulated, regular, or special method or plan of procedure that allows a couple to personalize a plan that meets each other's needs. Are you both committed to developing a plan?

_____

_____

_____

_____

4 What plan will the two of you put in place to accommodate and support the love and friendship that you profess for each other? List your areas of priority.

_____

_____

_____

_____

5 How would you define communication?

_____

_____

_____

_____

6 How do you prefer to communicate?

_____

_____

_____

_____

7 What thoughts would you like to share with your spouse about Me Time?

_____

_____

_____

_____

Lesson Three:
Single Minded – Mindset

1 How can a Single Minded Mindset ruin a marriage?

_____

_____

_____

_____

2 Discuss the following questions. You can pick one at a time during one of your sit downs together or discuss them all at once.

a) Where you are spiritually?
b) How you pay your bills? Online, due date, etc.
c) Synchronizing or the blending of your sleeping habits. Are you a night owl or an early bird?
d) The way or how often you clean?
e) How you do your laundry or keep your closet?
f) How you handle children if either of you have any?
g) How you cook or what you eat? No pork, Vegan, etc.
h) How do you deal with your family and friends?
i) What you do at and after work? Exercise, quiet time at home, etc.
j) The time and money that you spend on extracurricular activities? Do you have a budget for this?
k) Intimacy? A little, a lot, enjoy, etc.

Lesson Four:
I'm So Tired of Being Single

1 The definition of single is (of a person) not otherwise occupied; free to do something, or not currently involved in a sexual or romantic relationship. If we take a close look at the definition it does not look like gloom and doom. It looks like a person that is available for an opportunity. Are you open to taking advantage of this opportunity?

_____
_____
_____
_____

2 What would you like to fine tune in your life?

_____
_____
_____
_____

3 As you are in your preparation season will you commit to enjoy your single life while you can?

_____
_____
_____
_____

Lesson Five:
The Dynamics of Divorce

1

Divorce can cause
1. _____,
2. _____,
3. _____.

2

Who would be impacted by a divorce?
_____
_____
_____
_____

3

The top 10 culprits of divorce are:
a) _____
b) _____
c) _____
d) _____
e) _____
f) _____
g) _____
h) _____
i) _____
j) _____

Lesson Six:
Sacred Partnership

1 A partner is defined as a relationship resembling a legal partnership and usually involving close cooperation between parties, having specified and joint rights and responsibilities. What are two important points in that definition? _____

and _____ .

2 Why are the two important points you named above something that you should understand and focus on in your marriage?

_____

_____

_____

_____

3 Why is it important to know your spouse's family philosophy?

_____

_____

_____

_____

Lesson Seven:
Getting to Know Your Mate

1 Who should be the pilot _____
and who should be the copilot _____ ?

2 A marriage means that you are in flight. Once the plane is in flight, _____
IS GETTING OFF.

3 Love and planning cannot always avoid a storm or turbulence. Anything can happen. And you have to know that the person you now share your last name with is up for anything. How can that be achieved? How can two people know, as much as possible if they have found Mr. or Mrs. Anything?

_____

_____

_____

_____

_____

_____

_____

Lesson Eight:
Who Do You Love

1 What are the four types of attraction listed in this chapter?

a) _____

b) _____

c) _____

d) _____

2 _____ is key.

3 Make sure you _____ all of your bases.

Lesson Nine:
Mastering the Middle Ground

1

A _____ _____
is something that is spoken when the two of you are having a general conversation, while the two of you are joking or when you are telling a story to each other or to someone else.

_____

_____

_____

_____

2

The rule is: *It is your responsibility to discuss with your mate anything directly or indirectly spoken that is important to you.*
Is this something that you can commit to do?_____

3

The conversation should include the following:
   a) You want to share what you heard.
   b) They should in turn share what they said.
   c) You want to share what that meant to you.
   d) They should in turn share what it meant to them.
   e) What is our joint understanding or expectation on this topic?

_____

_____

Lesson Ten:
Relationship Building Blocks

1 What are the four relationship building blocks?

a) _____

b) _____

c) _____

d) _____

2 What does the word FAIR stand for?

_____

_____

_____

_____

3 What are the four overlooked triggers of conflict?

a) _____

b) _____

c) _____

d) _____

Lesson Eleven: The Numbers

1
In 2010 the divorce rate was _____ %, that means _____ % of marriages were successful. I want your marriage to end up in the _____%.

2
The fight is against the _____ or _____, the fight is not against your _____.

3
Have the _____ to ask the other not to give up on your marriage.

4
Is there a difference between the percentage of divorces in couples who have children or not?

_____

Lesson Twelve:
Stay Close to Each Other

1 Intimacy means something _____ to everyone so you want to discover what that means to each of you.

2 There is a difference between having an _____ for your spouse and having a _____.

3 Do you understand the difference between an attraction and a sexual appetite? _____

4 If so, please describe it in your own words.

_____

_____

_____

5 Have a conversation with each other about your personal sexual appetite. How often, how long and what you enjoy or dislike.

_____

_____

Tools Page

What Tools Have You Learned In This Chapter?

_____

_____

_____

_____

_____

_____

_____

_____

_____

_____

_____

_____

_____

_____

_____

_____

_____

_____

Total Capacity Maximizer

What is a Maximizer?

A maximizer is someone who has the insight and knowledge to evaluate others ability to succeed. The ability to go from nowhere to somewhere and build something from below average to above average. They can help to transform something from weak to strong or minute to large with dedication and commitment. Aggressively searching for the skills and talents that can be cultivated to achieve a desired result. Having the ability to recognize undeveloped potential and strength to produce excellence in the lives of others. When Dawn sees potential in others in any area of their life, she has a burning desire to share with them the tools and skills that she has developed to maximize her own life with the hope that it will maximize theirs. Having a keen eye for undeveloped skill, talent, potential, desire, ability, and gifting, she hones in on the areas that can be groomed and increased in an effort to produce excellence. Her goal is to take something average and make it superb, polishing it until it shines!

Experience: Corporate Trainer and Strategist

Dr. Dawn M. Harvey is Principal and Founder of CGI, LLC. which is the culmination of her speaking, training, and company leadership development experience. She is a published author, sought after speaker, corporate trainer and inventor. Dr. Harvey has over twenty five years of corporate and professional experience. She has worked with notable companies such as Boddie Noell Enterprises, Marriott, Federal Express, Legal Shield, Sisters for Sisters, Inc., Department of Health and Human Resources, Department of Transportation, HCDI, Washington Suburban Sanitary Commission and the National Organization of Black Women in Law Enforcement. Dawn has also obtained her Doctorate in Christian Theology. Dawn works extensively in ministry and is dedicated to the restoration and development of those that she comes into contact with.
Visit www.dicconline.com

Dr. Harvey has repeatedly proven her ability to develop, enhance and improve corporations, non-profit organizations, entrepreneurs, ministries, and individuals. Dr. Harvey has a proven track record in the implementation and strategic development vital to yielding impressive results. Dr. Harvey has the uncanny ability to identify strengths and weaknesses in an effort to improve a company or individuals performance. Her passion and commitment to support those who desire to achieve their goals no matter what the circumstances are, is evident as she trains throughout the country. The possibility that anyone, at anytime, anywhere, can make a decision to increase their capacity and maximize their life regardless of where they are, is what drives Dawn.

Dr. Harvey's flexible execution and training modules surpass expectation and yield long term results. Dr. Harvey's keen precision when training or coaching allows each team member to identify with their own personal ability and enhance the workforce and company. Before transitioning to entrepreneurship, Dr. Harvey exceeded corporate expectation and received numerous corporate and monetary awards for outstanding performance or idea implementation. She is known for the execution of strategic initiatives that impact the bottom line and increase the profit margin. Her ability to cultivate and develop skills and talents are displayed in the events and training you will experience with Dawn. Establishing goals, marking required targets and solidifying your commitment level are all viable as you implement the skills you will learn in each training session. Like an architect, she is a person who is professionally engaged in the design of goals and dreams. Having the willingness to push yourself beyond boundaries and limitations will accelerate your progress and advance your growth. These are the things that will assist you as you reach to achieve a higher capacity in your life to maximize your results. With a win, win mentality; it is Dr. Harvey's objective to positively impact and grow your company.

High Profile Tactics

Corporate Executives and High-profile clients rely on Dawn as a Confidential Advisor, Intercessor, and Confidant. With wisdom and a personal touch, Dawn has helped meet and resolve the private needs of those who desire non-disclosure assistance. Her approach to - Resolve Without Exposure allows each client to utilize any necessary services and resources privately.

Dawn Harvey Speaks

Dr. Harvey has a unique and attention grabbing delivery style that has been displayed in her consistent training career over the last 25 years. Her ability to tap into the climate in the room and address the real issues and needs of her audience has not only inspired many but provoked change. Dr. Harvey not only coaches and instructs from her years of training and education but from actually operating in the entrepreneurial process which includes launching, running, organizing and managing an enterprise or business. The combination of training and experience make for a priceless combination.

Dr. Harvey is available and may be requested for your next event as a keynote speaker, panelist, workshop facilitator, and television, news and radio segments.

Requested Trainings:

Embrace Your Greatness® "Celebrating the Ten Year Anniversary" - You have everything that you need to be great. There is no situation or circumstance that can deny the passion and drive of a person's true greatness. Greatness cannot and will not be denied.

Legacy Leadership – Foundational Leadership Teachings that stabilize a person, company or institution's growth and development, which in turn ensures its longevity.

Developing Maximized Potential – Identifying talent and potential with a game plan strategy to maximize the results.

From Zero to Six Figures – As it is said of old, "The Proof is In the Pudding." After over 25 years of corporate and personal facilitation and 14 years of entrepreneurship, Dr. Harvey delivers an applicable and beneficiary strategy to monetize your idea, product, service or talent.

It's Personal – An accurate and power packed teaching on defining and instituting your personal philosophy.

Contact Information

If this book has helped you or you have a story you would like to share about your relationship, please write us or visit www.strongestmarriagesinamerica.com. We would like to hear about your journey as a single person preparing for marriage, an engaged couple or a married couple. Our sponsors would love to see your stories and possibly be able to support you in your endeavors to become one of the Strongest Marriages in America. We would love to hear from you.

Invite Dr. Harvey to come and speak at your conference or event, you will never be the same.

All correspondence can be sent to:

SMIA
6715 Suitland Road
Morningside, MD 20746
(701)484-3303
Or email info@strongestmarriagesinamerica.com

CPSIA information can be obtained at www.ICGtesting.com
Printed in the USA
BVOW06s1943041016

464155BV00010B/18/P